What Is To Be Done?

For, ultimately, what did Machiavelli urge upon his readers, long before Chernyshevsky and Lenin, if not the problem and the question: What is to be done?

Louis Althusser, *The Future Lasts Forever*

What Is To Be Done?

Louis Althusser

Edited and Translated by G. M. Goshgarian

polity

Originally published in French as *Que Faire?* © Presses Universitaires de France/ Humensis, *Que Faire?*, 2018

This English edition © 2020 by Polity Press

Polity Press
65 Bridge Street
Cambridge CB2 1UR, UK

Polity Press
101 Station Landing
Suite 300
Medford, MA 02155, USA

ISBN-13: 978-1-5095-3860-7
ISBN-13: 978-1-5095-3861-4 (paperback)

A catalogue record for this book is available from the British Library.

Library of Congress Cataloging-in-Publication Data
Names: Althusser, Louis, 1918-1990, author. | Goshgarian, G. M., editor.
Title: What is to be done? / Louis Althusser ; edited and translated by G.M. Goshgarian.
Other titles: Que faire? English
Description: Cambridge, UK ; Medford, MA : Polity Press, [2020] | Originally published in French as Que Faire? in 2018 by PUF. | Includes bibliographical references and index.
| Summary: "A leading Marxist philosopher lays out his practical vision for political struggle"-- Provided by publisher.
Identifiers: LCCN 2020012866 (print) | LCCN 2020012867 (ebook) | ISBN 9781509538607 (hardback) | ISBN 9781509538614 (paperback) | ISBN 9781509538621 (epub) | ISBN 9781509544196 (adobe pdf)
Subjects: LCSH: Gramsci, Antonio, 1891-1937. | Revolutions. | Communism.
Classification: LCC HX289.7.G73 A7313 2020 (print) | LCC HX289.7.G73 (ebook) | DDC 335.43--dc23
LC record available at https://lccn.loc.gov/2020012866
LC ebook record available at https://lccn.loc.gov/2020012867

Typeset in 10.5 on 12pt Sabon
by Fakenham Prepress Solutions, Fakenham, Norfolk NR21 8NL
Printed and bound in Great Britain by TJ International Limited

The publisher has used its best endeavours to ensure that the URLs for external websites referred to in this book are correct and active at the time of going to press. However, the publisher has no responsibility for the websites and can make no guarantee that a site will remain live or that the content is or will remain appropriate.

Every effort has been made to trace all copyright holders, but if any have been overlooked the publisher will be pleased to include any necessary credits in any subsequent reprint or edition.

For further information on Polity, visit our website:
politybooks.com

Contents

Acknowledgements

G. M. Goshgarian thanks Nathalie Léger, director of the Institut mémoires de l'édition contemporaine, together with the rest of the Imec staff, the Arles Centre international de traducteurs littéraires, and François Boddaert, Fabio Bruschi, Jackie Épain, Luke Épain, Julie Le Men, Vittorio Morfino, Vanessa Roghi, Stefan Schomann, Laurie Tuller, and Fang Yan.

Note on the Text

The text on which the present translation is based, an unfinished manuscript titled *Que faire?* that Louis Althusser wrote in 1978, was first published in 2018 in an edition that I prepared for the Presses universitaires de France/Humensis. The French edition is based on a photocopy of a ninety-five-page typed manuscript bearing many corrections in Althusser's hand. This photocopy, four pages of which are defective, would appear to be the only copy of the text in Althusser's archives, housed in the Institut mémoires de l'édition contemporaine (Imec) in Caen. An appeal to Althusser's collaborators failed to turn up other copies of *Que faire?*

A list of notes has been preserved at the Imec along with the photocopied manuscript. They bear on passages of Antonio Gramsci's *Quaderni del carcere* (*Prison Notebooks*) quoted or referred to in *Que faire?* However, they contain no note markers pegging them to the text. Some of the notes contain brief comments, all of them in Italian; one includes a handwritten sentence that is not in Althusser's hand. The references to *Prison Notebooks* in the present edition are, without exception, taken from this list, which refers to the edition of the *Quaderni* published in 1975 under Valentino Gerratana's general editorship. Where possible, I have replaced the references to the Italian edition with references to published English translations. I have also inserted note markers at what seemed to be the right places.

All other notes to the text are mine, with the exception of one note by Althusser. I am responsible for the division of the text into chapters as well as the chapter titles. The general title is Althusser's. A few minor errors on Althusser's part have been silently corrected.

1

The 'What' in 'What Is To Be Done?'

What is to be done?

That old question of Lenin's, which initiated the construction and the practices of the Bolshevik Party, is not, for a communist who knows Marxist theory, a question like any other. It is a political question. What is to be done to help to orient and organize the workers' and the people's class struggle so that it carries the day against the bourgeois class struggle?

We should weigh all the words in this simple question.

What is to be done to help to orient *and* organize the workers' and the people's class struggle? It can be seen that orientation, or the political line, *comes before* organization. This is to affirm the primacy of the political line over the party, and the construction and organization of the party *as a function* of the political line.

What is to be done to help to orient and organize the workers' and the people's class struggle? It can be seen that orientation (the line) and organization (the party) *depend* on the workers' and the people's class struggle. Thus the party is the instrument of the political line, and the political line itself is the expression of the current workers' and people's class struggle, that is, of its tendency, antagonistic to the tendency of the bourgeois class struggle.

Everything depends, therefore, on the 'concrete analysis of the concrete situation'[1] of the current tendency of the workers' and people's class struggle in its antagonism to the bourgeois class struggle. Hence everything depends on the concrete analysis of this *antagonism*, which constitutes the bourgeois class as a dominant, exploiting class and, simultaneously, the working class as a dominated, exploited class.

If it is true that Marx upheld, at least with respect to the capitalist mode of production, the thesis of the primacy of contradiction over the contraries, that is, of the class struggle over the classes, *then it is this antagonism itself* which must comprise the object of 'the concrete analysis of the concrete situation'. Otherwise, we lapse into 'vulgar sociology'. Otherwise, we will analyse the bourgeois class on the one hand and the working class on the other, in the belief that we can come to know them separately. It is as if we believed that we could understand a game of football by 'analysing' the line-ups of the teams, not their *match-ups*, without which there would not be a single football team on earth.[2]

When we say 'primacy of contradiction over the contraries', 'primacy of the class struggle over the classes', we are merely stating an abstract principle. For we have to go to the field, in the 'concrete', to see, *in detail*, what forms this antagonism historically takes, and what historical forms it confers on the classes that it constitutes. In order to understand the significance and fecundity of these principles, then, we cannot dispense with going 'to the field' and analysing things down to the smallest detail.

How can we carry out this 'concrete analysis of a concrete situation'? How can we learn in detail what goes on, for example, in the conditions of life, work, and exploitation of a metalworker or petrochemical worker, a worker on a 'family' farm or an industrial farm, a rail worker, bank clerk, social security employee, and so on?

Some people believe that it is enough to address an appeal to those involved, to ask them to talk about their lives, their jobs, how they are exploited, and the like. That is what *L'Humanité Dimanche*, for example, has done by appealing to all its readers to whom the word applies to tell it about 'poverty'.[3] And the newspaper has received a considerable number of letters, which are, incidentally, slumbering in its managing editor's office.[4] Well and good. The workers are writing, they are saying a great many interesting, incredible, overwhelming things. This can provide *some* material for a concrete analysis. It is not a concrete analysis.

Some people believe that it is enough to head for the field, without preparation, and interview the workers. Either they ask them questions (but everyone knows that spontaneous questions aren't spontaneous, that they are biased by the 'ideas' that the person asking them has in mind) and the workers say what they *feel like* saying; or else they arrange matters so as to let the workers talk, interfering as little as possible themselves. In that case too, however, the workers say what they feel like saying. Assuming they say *everything* they know, one thing is certain: they always know much more (or much less) about things than they think they do. They do not say this 'much more', because they do not know that they know it. As for this 'much less', it is masked by what they think they do know.[5] These 'interviews' too can provide *some* material for a concrete analysis. They are not a concrete analysis.

One cannot dispense with going to the field and listening carefully to the workers – but neither can one dispense with *preparing* for this encounter. It is not a question of psychological preparation for the purpose of establishing 'good personal contact' (of the kind that 'the human relations approach' manufactures). It is a question of *theoretical* and *political* preparation. That is why it is possible to say that *a concrete analysis and the Marxist theory* or *political consciousness of the conditions for knowledge* are one and the same thing. All that differs is the *scale* of the object.

Lenin was in the habit of saying that the working class must take the greatest possible account of what goes on outside it, in the bourgeois class, not just to know itself, but to constitute itself as a conscious class (that is, as a class endowed with a party that orients, unifies and organizes its struggle). It cannot be satisfied with knowing what is going on in its own domain, that is, with knowing itself; it must also see and understand what is going on on the other side. This is not a question of simple curiosity; it is a question of grasping the two poles of the antagonism at the same time *in order to be able to grasp the antagonism as that which constitutes the two poles,* in order to grasp the class struggle as that which constitutes the classes by dividing them into classes. Otherwise, the working class will be penned within its own horizon, that of its exploitation, of its revolts with no morrow, doubled by its utopian dreams; and it will, in this captivity, be subject to all the pressures and manoeuvres of the bourgeois class struggle.

To succeed in grasping the antagonism, to succeed in understanding the mechanism of this class struggle that divides the classes into classes, mere 'self-consciousness' is not enough. Italian television recently interviewed Alfa Romeo workers at their workplace.[6] These were vanguard workers with extraordinarily high consciousness. The audience saw everything they did at work; the workers said everything they knew. They were workers in a separate workshop who held a simple place in Alfa Romeo's immense labour process. Isolated though they were, in their shop, in their work, they had nevertheless managed to arrive at an idea of the structure and mechanisms of the process of production in their plant, and not just the labour process in their own plant, but also the subcontracting going on outside it, and even Alfa Romeo's economic and financial policies, its investments, markets, and so on. These workers had even acquired – this is extremely unusual – a certain consciousness of *the effects produced on them* by this system: on their own working conditions, their exploitation, the relation between this exploitation and the conditions for the reproduction of their own labour-power (their housing, their families – the wife and children – school, social security, transport, their car, and so on). They had even understood, to a certain extent – this is still more surprising – that their isolation as well as the ignorance of company policies in which the monopoly Alfa Romeo keeps its workers, including ignorance of its organization and its division of labour, were *part and parcel of the conditions of their exploitation*, since this isolation and ignorance were *one of the forms* of the bourgeois class struggle, intended to keep them from attaining *accurate* collective consciousness, and thus from carrying out effective industrial action or political action.

Thus these workers had gone a very long way in 'developing their consciousness' [*dans leur 'prise de conscience'*][7] – and I insist that what is involved here is a case of exceptional 'consciousness', incomprehensible outside the context of the struggles of the Italian metalworkers, who have, for years, ventured well beyond the bounds of traditional trade union demands (the defence of wage levels, the fight against speed-up, and so on) in order to intervene in the organization of the labour process and workers' control over it, and even in the investment policies of the trust that employs them. In France, we are far, very far, from having an example of this kind.

Yet the very same workers who displayed this extraordinary capacity for analysis ran up against an insuperable problem. While they knew what was going on in their plant and trust, they had no comparable idea of what was really going on at Fiat, that is, in the same branch of production; and they had *absolutely no idea* of what was going on in the other branches of production in Italy: metalworking, textiles, the petrochemical industry, mining, agriculture, transport, the financial trusts and the trusts that control commercial distribution, and so on. It is, however, absolutely impossible to arrive at an idea of what *determines* what goes on at Alfa Romeo unless one has as comprehensive an idea as possible of Alfa Romeo's *position* not just in the production of automobiles, and the market for them, but also in metalworking, textiles, the plastics industry, the petrochemical industry and the rubber industry – industries directly relevant to automobile production, because they provide the automobile industry with their finished products, which serve as the raw material for the construction of vehicles. And it is absolutely impossible to grasp what determines the existence and importance of automobile production in a nation's production without understanding the specific *place* that automobile production holds in economic production overall, that is, in the ensemble of existing branches of production. This place, in turn, can be grasped only if one is prepared to consider the competition among capitals seeking the highest possible rate of profit, which explains why capital is invested in the automotive sector (rather than others) and, at the same time, the place that this investment holds in the bourgeoisie's overall economic strategy, inseparable from the bourgeois class struggle.

While it may seem surprising, studies have proven that the *mass* production of automobiles, which were once an object of curiosity and a luxury item for the rich – that the production of automobiles at comparatively low prices *for the masses*, hence *for the workers*, a mass production consciously inaugurated by Ford in America, *involved a complete overhaul of the previous strategy of the bourgeois class struggle.*

At one time, a factory-owner built housing for workers around his factory. This was common practice not just in mining (settlements of miners' cottages), but in metal-working and textiles as well (workers' estates). This solution had its advantages: the workers did not need transport (= wasted time) and arrived at their jobs fresh and rested in the morning. The boss had his own shops, schools, church and parish priest on the premises. He could exploit his little world twice over, both at work and also by selling it clothing and the means of subsistence. Above all, he could keep a close eye on his little world, which he had at his mercy thanks to exploitation at work, dependency and profits in consumption, and his priests and schoolteachers.

This double concentration in one and the same place – concentration in the labour process and concentration in the maintenance and reproduction of labour-power – had, however, serious disadvantages as well. The first was that it was impossible to augment the workforce without investing in the construction of housing, and so on. The boss ran up against this first limit and, above all, a second: this double concentration multiplied exchanges between workers and lent them formidable force in the struggle.

Marx stresses the role that the *concentration* of workers in the production process plays in 'raising consciousness' of class interests and in the organization of collective struggles.[8] When concentration in the labour process goes hand-in-hand with concentration in the habitat, when workplace and habitat are practically identical, and when *none but* the workers in a factory live together in the same residential zone, it is easy to imagine the explosive effects that this double concentration can have on 'raising consciousness' and on struggles. It is no accident that, in the history of workers' struggles, miners were long in the vanguard, followed by dockers and metalworkers, and then by textile workers.

In the face of this grave peril, which jeopardized its exploitation, *the bourgeoisie altered its strategy.* It abandoned its old practice of building 'workers' estates' around the factory, gave up all the advantages that it had reaped from this, and took a different tack.

More and more workers were needed. To recruit them, there was no depending on the kind of 'urban planning' that provided accommodation in workers' estates, miners' cottage settlements, and the like. It was necessary to be able to recruit any worker anywhere at will, even if he lived at some distance or even very far away; and it was also necessary to be able to 'play' on market fluctuations so as to augment or diminish the workforce in a particular branch of production or shift it from one branch of production to another. Workforce 'mobility' became a sine qua non for the development of imperialist capitalism, for its 'play' on capital investments and transfers of those investments. Capital had finally to be completely liberated from the old fetters represented by investments of fixed capital in workers' estates located around the factory. *The mobility of capital, subject to the search for maximal profit* (on the basis of the average rate of profit), necessitated *the mobility of the workforce.* Concretely, this meant that the workforce was freed of the obligation to live in a particular habitat tied to proximity to the factory. It became obvious that – a reason inseparable from the first reason (for, when the bourgeoisie sets out to reap the greatest possible profit from exploitation, which is class struggle, it must simultaneously ensure the greatest possible social and political *security* for that exploitation) – it became obvious that, in order to counter the workers' struggle that was emerging as a result of this double concentration, *workers had to be scattered as widely as possible.* It was already more than enough that they were brought together in the concentration of the labour process. They should not, to make things worse, *also* be brought together around the factory in a workers' estate!

These are not imaginary variations, but facts, and I am by no means arbitrarily imputing motives to the bourgeoisie. We have a great many texts, declarations and studies written by its own specialists that *prove that it was perfectly conscious of the class character of its 'turnabout' on the political matter of workers' housing* – that it was *conscious* of the dangers this 'turnabout' was meant to stave off and of the effects it expected from this turnabout.

Naturally, this 'turnabout' on the matter of the workers' habitat, which left the choice of their accommodations entirely up to them (go live wherever you like, I don't care to know anything about it), simultaneously exposed workers to the logic of a whole series of complex, seemingly aleatory processes in which urban ground rent played the leading role, alongside the most cynical politics (Haussmann demolishing workers' neighbourhoods in the centre of Paris in order to open up broad avenues in which post-1848 rifles and artillery could 'work wonders'). This contributed to driving the mass of workers into the suburbs, which had gradually gained ground at the expense of cultivated fields. Finance capital, urban ground rent, and politics thus succeeded in transforming the class characteristics of the neighbourhoods of capitalism's new urban planning. Pushed into distant suburbs, the workers found what accommodations they could. When the bourgeoisie realized that, concentrated as they were in production, they were still too dangerous, it set out to 'change their attitude'; that is, put baldly, to invite them to desert the class struggle *by interesting them in proprietorship* – by allowing them to buy their little houses and gardens in the suburbs. The result was the politics of the detached house, explicitly conceived of as, and, without the least dissimulation, openly declared to be, *essential to the depoliticization of the working class*. The result was the working-class property owner, with all the hours given over to do-it-yourself chores in house and garden, far from any 'café' and, what is more, stuck with long-term loans and stuck in his little family. What better guarantee for capitalism could anyone dream of?

This is where we come back to the automobile. In the grand transformation of the bourgeois politics of labour-power, the automobile was clearly and consciously conceived of by Ford, who pioneered mass production of it, *as a product for the masses, hence for the workers*. It was conceived of as an indispensable means of enabling workers – living wherever they happened to find lodging and therefore, usually, far from the factory, and even farther than from the factory nearest them, perhaps, if their first lay-off, and so forth – to transport themselves from their homes to the factory gates and present themselves there about as fresh as they would have been if they had lived in the immediate vicinity. It is of no importance that there exist factories for the rich (Lancia, Ferrari) and factories such as Alfa Romeo, somewhat more specialized in cars that are, as a rule, beyond ordinary workers' [*ouvriers*] means (and even that no longer holds since the Alfasud). Cars render the same services to other workers [*travailleurs*] – white-collar workers, supervisory personnel, and so on – who also live far from the company where they work. What is important is that Ferrari, Lancia and even Alfa Romeo exist *on the basis constituted by*

Fiat and its analogues (General Motors, Ford, Citroën, Welter-Meunier, and so on), that is to say, a gigantic imperialist enterprise, implanted throughout the world, *whose automotive sector is all but exclusively devoted to turning out mass-produced cars for mass consumption: in other words, popular cars which workers can usually afford.*

This reality, which some fail to perceive even today – namely, that the automobile is an integral part of the means of transport for labour-power, that is, of its maintenance and availability as exploited labour, just as the means of transport serve, among other things, to transport commodities to market, thus making possible the 'commodity's transformation into a commodity'[9] – this reality finds its explanation not in 'technical progress' or 'rising productivity', but in the history of a phenomenal about-face in the strategy of the bourgeois class struggle. *This is something that not even the most conscious workers at Alfa Romeo could know.* Not only could they not get beyond the limits of their own company, whose structure and mechanism they understood quite well; not only could they not know as much about what was going on at Fiat (whose investment strategy and strategy of multiproduction on a global scale was beyond their ken); not only could they not know what was going on in other branches of Italian domestic production; they were also obviously unaware of the crucial role that the mass production of cars had played in capitalism's strategic transformation with regard to labour-power in the context of the bourgeois class struggle.

There we have, then, what happened and what failed to in this extraordinary Italian television documentary in which workers at Alfa Romeo talked about their work, their exploitation, their capitalist company, the mechanisms of its production process and of its investment policy, and also about its way of waging the class struggle in the factory, the riposte to which was an exceptionally vigorous working-class struggle.

What happened was *what one saw and heard.* One saw, on TV, workers at work, and heard them say what they knew, what they had, in the course of their struggles, become conscious of. And what they said was staggering. The fact that they had, by themselves, that is, in their trade union struggle, acquired such consciousness, such knowledge, showed that they knew as much as the best of the factory's managers and engineers and that, at least on certain points, they knew more.

However, one *saw only* what one saw, and that does not go very far: a man at work is an able intelligence of a high order, but no more. And one *heard only* what they *said*, what they had succeeded in learning. All that was missing was the rest … the rest, that is to say, the whole of the general system governing the concrete forms and methods of the *bourgeois class struggle as a whole* in its *antagonism* to the workers' class struggle, which comes down to this simple *fact* that seems to go without saying, yet is enigmatic, like everything that 'goes without saying': *Why is the production of automobiles based entirely on their mass production, hence on production for the masses? Why, in other words, do workers have automobiles, hence a need for automobiles?* You thought, perhaps, that they bought them for the fun of it or to go for rides with the family on Sunday, to go see their friends? *Why automobiles for workers?* The workers at Alfa Romeo did not ask this simple question, which commands everything. They could not ask it.

For it is not by observing or even analysing the work of workers on the job, or even the labour process, or even the company's investment policy, or even its class struggle policy in the plant, that we can arrive at the theoretical principles that make it possible to understand, in its core and its manifestations, the fundamental antagonism of the class struggle that divides the classes into classes. To do that, we must have recourse to the only theory that has taken this problem into account, and has taken it seriously, and has actually, concretely solved it, in a form that practice verifies every day: Marxist theory. *Thus there is no concrete analysis of the concrete situation without minimal mastery of Marxist theory.* This mastery is essential to understanding the general system in which things happen. This system encompasses, today, the global capital market, as well as the multinationals, their 'policy' [*leur 'politique'*] of shifting investments as a function of the most poorly paid labour force, of their search for, and conquest of, sources of raw materials, of fluctuations in their prices, of this or that country's alarming or reassuring 'political situation', and so on. In order to understand *the place occupied by a particular labour process in which a particular worker in a particular branch of production is engaged*, one has to understand the mechanism of this system, at least in its broad outlines.

The same mastery, however, is essential, quite as essential, to acquiring the ability to '*listen correctly*' [*avoir une 'écoute' juste*] when face-to-face with workers talking about their life and work. For, to be able to listen to them, those listening must know which questions to ask and which not to; they must know how to put what the workers say into relation with what the workers themselves do not know about the effects that the general process has on their own condition; finally, and above all, they must be open to learning, by way of this relation, what they do not know and what the workers do, but without knowing that they know it, and yet say after all – albeit obliquely, indirectly, and even in their omissions and silences.

The fact that workers know more about things than they know, or less about things than they know, brings out a reality with which Marxist theory is well acquainted and which it has revealed to us: the *effects of ideology*. The conditions of life, work, exploitation, struggle, and the reproduction of labour-power are not things in plain sight that we can observe the way we observe what goes on in a train station. Even if, as Marx remarks, the machinery of big industry reduces workers to the state of appendages to itself,[10] human beings are not 'machine animals'.[11] They are, rather, 'ideological animals'.[12] They have what we call 'ideas' about themselves, their work and the world.

These ideas can occur to them in scattered order, according to the chance occurrences [*les hasards*] of their experience; yet they always end up grouped together under general systems of ideas that have a certain cohesion, in the absence of complete coherency – systems known as *ideologies*. They always *end up* grouped together under these ideologies, because they were *already* grouped together under them *beforehand*, and because 'the chance occurrences of experience' are, more often than not, simply the form ideologies take in order to impose themselves on social individuals. The ideologies are not the sum of individuals' 'ideas'; they are 'systems' that are rigid or supple or, usually, both. Ideologies are not 'ideas' pure and simple (something that does not exist at all in this form); but, since they always bear a relationship to practice and always inspire a certain system of *practical* judgements and attitudes, they must be understood in their *body*,[13] hence also in the activity of the body.[14]

Yes, ideologies have bodies, from which they emanate, just as they bear on *bodies*.[15] These bodies are 'institutions', above all the state and its various ideological apparatuses (the legal system, school system, political system, trade-union system [*système syndical*],[16] religious, familial, medical, informational and cultural systems, etc.). A fierce ideological class struggle between the dominant ideology (that of the dominant class) and the dominated ideologies is waged in the ensemble of these ideological regions.

All this, which seems to take us very far from the worker, brings us straight back to him. For he is *the site* where complex ideologies *confront each other*, down to his very body, ideologies whose antagonism is 'naturally' concealed from him. The state and the whole of its general ideological system, as well as the capitalists and their whole ideological system for internal use, are constantly suggesting 'ideas' to the worker in which he can recognize himself [*se reconnaître*], 'ideas' about wages as the price of labour, about social advancement, about profit-sharing, about voluntary task-sharing, about the distinction between the economy (production) and politics, about the moral values in which he must steep himself if he wants to be a good father and family man, and about the school system that will ensure his children's future, when it is not the Church that christens them, catechizes them, and tells them as it does him about life eternal as recompense for tribulations in this world. This impressive system of systems, which is neither formal nor formalizable (Marxism has nothing to do with 'systems theory', which today represents the theoretical ideology of the vanguard of imperialism's ideological class struggle), possesses sufficient power of intimidation and, sometimes, sufficient compensatory charms, to make the workers forget that they are mere appendages of the machine, in other words, the ones exploited by capitalism. The workers, however, also have before their eyes the real condition that is reserved for them; and, in the event that they revolt and that their revolt is informed by organized struggle, *other ideas* occur to them: those that expose the previous ideas as mystifications; those that speak to them about the reality of the class struggle and the need to unite to change their working conditions and this society that incessantly engenders them.

What I have said about the subject here is extremely schematic. How can one deal with it in a few lines? Yet a few lines suffice to bring out the fact that workers who *talk* about their working and living conditions do not talk about them like entomologists, but like human beings who are *either* more or less subject to the concrete forms that the dominant ideology produces in order to respond to their precise preoccupations, *or* who are more or less emancipated from them, and rendered, by this emancipation, more or less conscious of their working conditions and conditions of exploitation, with all their repercussions on the reproduction of their labour-power. We can now understand the statement, which has doubtless remained enigmatic up to now, that workers can *know more about things than they think they do*, but also, for this case too presents itself, can *know less about things than they think they do*.

Paradoxically, it is not always when they are the most 'conscious' that they autómatically know more about things than they think they do. For they can then be blinded, in a way, by the elementary truths of the 'consciousness' they have acquired: we see this in militants in whom the abc's of consciousness become a kind of absolute knowledge that blinds them to a big part of their own and, above all, their comrades' condition. These militants take self-consciousness for knowledge, and their self-consciousness stands in the way of their knowledge. On the other hand, it happens that workers who make no pretence to possessing any special 'consciousness', if only because they do not belong to a trade union or political organization, actually know much more about things than they think they do. They do not take their self-consciousness for knowledge and that consciousness does not automatically stand in the way of their knowledge. A serious concrete analysis has to attend to these differences and paradoxes.

Such paradoxes are not just natural curiosities; *they are of very great political importance.* For, in the Marxist tradition, it is on these paradoxes that the primacy of the masses over the classes, and the primacy of the masses and classes over the class struggle organizations – the trade union and party – are founded.[17] It is not at all a matter of lapsing into a cult of the masses; it is a matter of being extremely attentive to the workers' level of consciousness, in the awareness that their level of consciousness and, a fortiori, of *knowledge* does not necessarily correspond to the level they think they have reached, hence to their self-consciousness. By the primacy of the masses over the classes, of the masses and classes over the trade union and party, the Marxist tradition means to express a great many other things as well, but, with respect to the matter at hand, it designates, in the form of a warning to the wise, the simple fact that the workers do not escape the ideological struggle, hence the domination of the dominant ideology, as well as the fact that every form of trade union or political consciousness is constantly in danger of taking itself for the whole truth unless it acknowledges that workers who are not organized and are therefore, in principle, less conscious can, in their silence, know a great deal more about things than those who speak a little too soon on their behalf.

We may now broach the hardest question, the one that is contained in the 'What' of 'What is to be done?' Before this question, however, there is another, just as hard, that is contained *in the very fact of asking the question.* We can legitimately ask *to whom* the political question 'What is to be done?' is addressed, to whom it *can possibly* be addressed. It would be too facile to answer that, since it is political, it is addressed to people who already know what politics, what political action, is, and who, consequently, possess the political consciousness to ask themselves, in a given situation, 'What is to be done?' Such people, this answer would run, are already militants who have acquired more or less extensive experience of organization and struggle, and who possess sufficient consciousness to understand that the class struggle has reached a critical point for the working class, that the working class can no longer, for example, continue with its old organization, its old line, its old practices. Under these conditions, the assumption is, they will ask themselves 'What is to be done?', like Lenin in 1903. They will put the question to themselves, as militants (more or less) conscious of the historical deadlock or crisis of the workers' class struggle organizations. Lenin, on this view, simply lent an ear to the workers' question and took it up in his turn, throwing it into the sharpest possible relief and giving it as much force and play as possible, but with the advantage (over the workers) that he suggested concrete answers to their question: it would be necessary to found a new organization, and it would be formed around a *newspaper* serving as the means of unifying the existing, but scattered, revolutionary 'circles'. This organization would have to maintain relations of such-and-such a kind with the workers' movement and the peasants' movement; it would have to conduct such-and-such a unitary-popular class struggle against the feudal/bourgeois class struggle and its instrument, Czarism; and, in this struggle, which would long remain clandestine, the party would have to be organized in such-and-such a way (a very strict democratic centralism), with a sizeable nucleus of 'professional revolutionaries', etc.

On this hypothesis, *a leader* takes up the question that
militants who are already conscious are asking themselves
and, on the basis of Marxist theory, enriched by the
objective demands of the hour, and on the basis of the
objective conditions of the existing class struggle and
also of what are known as 'subjective' conditions (the
existing level and forms of organization, which realize
the masses' and the militants' 'consciousness' and serve as
their measure), he gives very precise concrete answers to
the question 'What is to be done?' Taken together, these
answers comprise an entire system of principles of theory,
orientation, organization and action (for a 'long-term'
struggle), and, at the same time, the corresponding slogans
(for *immediate* action).

I insist on this point. Formally, we can recognize a
theoretically and politically responsible Marxist response
to the question 'What is to be done?' if we attend to the
fact that it *necessarily* has the dimension just mentioned,
a future-oriented dimension bearing on the 'long term'
of the workers' class struggle, which the one who asks
this question in public takes up in his turn. This future-
oriented dimension is what is called the response of
'strategy' or of the *'political line'* and, *simultaneously*, of
the theoretical, organizational, ideological and practical
means required to carry out this line in the struggle: for
example, in the case of France, the line of the Union of the
People of France,[18] cemented by the Union of the Left[19]
and the means that ought to correspond to it.

To be responsible, however, the Marxist response will
include, in addition to responses concerning the 'long
term' and, therefore, the strategy and 'line', responses
for *immediate action*: what might be called, at the limit,
'slogans'. Naturally, these 'slogans', to be applied straight
away or in the near future, do not constitute responses of
a kind completely different from the strategic responses,
since, on the contrary, it is only possible to conceive of
them, hence to state them, hence to propose them to party
(or trade union) militants on the basis of the strategic
responses, and therefore as a function of the 'long-term
struggle', which must take the greatest possible account

of all the elements of the objective situation and the dominant tendency in their antagonism.

For example, a slogan such as 'Fight foreclosures!' (cited by Georges Marchais in his report)[20] is undoubtedly *an immediate slogan*; but, as a slogan, it takes its place in the 'long-term line' of a class strategy of defence and unification of the popular masses in their struggle against imperialist exploitation. It paves the way, at its level, in the field – 'one step at a time, setting one stone on another' (G. Marchais), through a direct defence of French and immigrant workers, retirees with modest incomes, and other 'poor people' – for the strategic objective of helping them to unite in the struggle for 'democratic change' and, later, for socialism.

Similarly, a slogan such as 'Let us call on the metal-workers of the Lorraine region to fight for nationalization of the steel industry!'[21] – where the state guzzles billions that 'go to waste'[22] – is a slogan that is *both* immediate *and also* for the near future. This slogan too quite obviously takes its place in a 'long-term line' for the defence of an entire category of workers in an entire branch of production, with a view to paving the way, here again 'step by step', for the unification of the workers in their struggle to achieve clear strategic objectives, namely, popular union (or the Union of the People of France), of which 'the Union of the Left is the cement' (G. Marchais).

Formally speaking, this slogan is perfectly correct; but the question arises as to whether the 'objective' conditions for its application have been met. The 'subjective' conditions (the workers' determination to save their jobs at all costs, the trade union's and the party's determination) certainly have been met. The objective conditions, however, which not just a 'strategic line', but also every 'slogan' deriving from it must take into account, are, it must be said, problematic – not only because the bourgeoisie, victorious on 19 March,[23] surely has no 'intention', *as part of its own long-term strategy*, of nationalizing the steel industry, but also because, if a class really wanted to nationalize the steel industry, it would today, no matter which class is in power, run up against the tremendous problems created by the international competition, which is capable of flooding the *French* market with metallurgical products at a price thirty to fifty per cent lower than the French price of production, given the state of France's industrial equipment (and therefore its technical productivity), its wages and, in the final account, the *rate of profit* that the capitalists of the steel industry aim to obtain on the French market for metal production (since the market abroad has already been captured by Japan's and other countries' low-cost production).

For, if the capitalists of the steel industry do not obtain this rate of profit, currently lower in metallurgy than in other branches of French production, they will be tempted to abandon steel-making and, despite the very considerable difficulties involved, to convert their fixed capital (practically speaking, this is all but impossible: neither mines nor even blast furnaces can be converted!), look to other types of production, or, quite simply, arrange to be financed by the state, as is their habit. When a shop or, a fortiori, a whole branch of capitalist production arranges to be 'financed' by the state, what is in question is always, by way of state loans and thus taxes, such-and-such an amount of money (tens of billions of new francs) levied on the surplus value extorted from all productive workers [*travailleurs*], hence, first and foremost, from the working class [*la classe ouvrière*], not the capitalist class.

This example shows that it is sometimes relatively easy, or even quite easy, to 'derive' immediate slogans from the 'long-term strategic line' – for example, 'Fight foreclosures!', 'Defend workers' purchasing power!', 'Fight to extend democracy!' (proportional representation, defence and extension of trade union rights, recognition of political rights in the workplace) – and to achieve unity with the toiling peasantry, urban petty bourgeoisie, intellectuals and others in all possible forms and on the occasion of every concrete struggle. In contrast, it is often hard, or even very hard, to 'derive' certain slogans directly from a 'strategic line' that is in itself correct when the objective conditions for carrying these slogans into practice depend *directly*, in their turn, *on conditions that the 'political*

line' itself has not seriously taken into account. When
the political line has failed to take these conditions into
account, when it has not, in other words, recognized the
existence of these conditions and concretely analysed them,
it is an illusion to believe that a slogan, even one 'derived'
from a formally correct political line, will by some miracle
be able to do that 'political line's' work for it. This goes to
show that, at the limit, a slogan may be false even when it
derives from a formally correct political line.

This is plainly a limit situation in which the leadership
of a trade union or party has not done its job of '*concrete
analysis of a concrete situation*', or has done it only by
halves, from a distance and from on high, in the name of a
vague 'theory' that it is satisfied to apply. This is currently
the case of the French Communist Party and a good many
other communist parties.

The PCF has thus, for years, 'decided' from on high
what concrete reality should be, without conducting a
truly serious, in-depth concrete analysis. Rather, it has
contented itself with *applying*, to the simple, manifest and,
consequently, superficial phenomena of the 'concrete',
the truth of a 'theory' that is either artificial, or in part
arbitrary, or inexact and inadequate, albeit partially true
– a 'theory' that it has adopted for reasons of theoretical
legitimization of its 'political line'.

I mean the theory of State Monopoly Capitalism, as it
is called.[24] The Party thought that 'applying' a theory thus
constructed to visible 'concrete reality' would provide it
with authentic knowledge of that 'concrete reality'. Party
functionaries or other Communists have accordingly
produced, setting out from the theory of 'Stamocap',
an abundance of so-called 'concrete analyses' of 'the
social classes in France', or 'needs', or the University,
or science ('the scientific and technical revolution'), or
culture, and so on. There is some truth in these works,
but they are not genuinely theoretical studies: it would
be child's play to demonstrate this, as everyone knows
or suspects. There is a very long list of them, and if the
CDLP[25] is floundering, the poor sales figures of these
mediocre books are surely part of the reason: they have

not interested serious readers and are stacked up in their publishers' basements.

This public failure, one example of many, clearly indicates the road not to take: that of the mere *application* of a theory to the concrete. I do not just mean the application of a theory that is false or skewed by false premises; I mean the application of a theory in general, a *true* theory included. If you take Marxist theory, which you assume to be true, and, having decided to apply it to the concrete, wait for this 'application' to generate the truth of the concrete itself, you're in for a long wait. For this operation of *application* presupposes a completely *false* idea *of Marxist theory itself.*

If you apply a pre-existing theory to the concrete in order to know that concrete, you necessarily assume that the theory already contains in itself, if only in embryo, but in any case *in principle, the truth of the concrete* that you pretend to expect from the *application* of the theory. If you accept this position and generalize it, you postulate that Marxist theory possesses, in itself and in advance, in theoretical form, the truth of everything that can present itself in the world in the form of the 'concrete'. I am not here engaging in a sophistical critique; I am stating things as they are. In principle, this whole procedure is quite simple (even if it usually takes extremely complicated forms, precisely in order to mask its imposture). If Marxist theory is, in advance, the truth of the whole of the concrete, that is, of every concrete situation, that is, of everything new and unforeseen that can happen in history (and, for twenty years now, we have had our share and then some as far as the unforeseen and the unimaginable go!), this means that it is not a theory 'of a scientific' or 'operational' kind (the word doesn't much matter), but an absolute philosophy that knows everything, *absolutely everything, in advance*, because it is the 'science of first and last principles',[26] as a formula of Aristotle's has it – a formula that says just what it means.

The absurdity of such a pretension leaps to the eye right away when we consider two points: to begin with, the fact that the 'concrete' – that which people experience and that in which they react, revolt or submit, in which they act or resign themselves to things – constantly changes and never repeats itself. This is a basic truth that not just historians, who work on change, even when they appeal to certain major stabilities to explain it, but also ordinary mortals know well. The same sun rises every morning, bodies always fall the same way, blood always circulates (barring pathological disorders) in the same circulatory system, and so on. In social life, however, even in the great stabilities of the great empires of immobile history, *there is always something that is always in the process of changing*. In any case, while there is room for debate about the immobility of certain modes of production that reproduce themselves as they are, practically without change, and about the societies that stem from them, it is plain that *in the society we know*, at least, the capitalist mode of production, everything is always in the process of changing.

Not only does such-and-such a technical invention transform the material bases of such-and-such a branch of production (transport, for example, which has gone from the steam engine to electrical energy and chemical energy – jet planes and rockets), or create a new one (petroleum and its countless derivatives coming after coal and its derivatives; the electronic components that are creating an utterly unprecedented form of communication and, with the computer, providing means of organizing the process of production in detail, while anticipating the circulation and sale of products in extraordinarily complex situations), but, above all, the forms of the reproduction of production are, in capitalism, always 'expanded'. (Capitalism always discovers, in its crises, means of taking a new lease on life, as it did in the 1929 crisis, thanks, among other things, to war, a typical form of resolution of imperialism's worst crises.) These expanded forms of reproduction are by no means *technical* forms, in which case there would be no understanding why they have to be expanded; they are, in the last instance, *forms of the class struggle* that the national and global imperialist bourgeoisie wages against its domestic working class and the peoples of the world recently liberated from political oppression.

Thus *the concrete* is not just *that which changes* (at least in our society); it is that which is changing *at top speed and ever faster.* The fact that our century is the century of speed finds its explanation in the imperatives of the bourgeois class struggle – to make capital circulate as fast as possible in order to extract as much surplus value as possible, to reduce the time of circulation of the different fractions of capital to a minimum in order to increase surplus value proportionately, to step up the pace of the labour process in order to extract as much surplus value as possible, to realize the maximum amount of surplus value with the capital invested in machines, utilizing them as fully as possible before being forced to replace them when competitors bring new, less expensive and more productive machines onto the market, and so on. The speed of our century, which has even become a literary theme and a theme of lamentation, is not due, in the last instance, to the automobile (speed limits on the autoroutes), air-plane or rocket, but to this acceleration of the cycle of the expanded reproduction of capital, which is inseparable from the intensification of exploitation by the capitalist class struggle – something that confers all its meaning on the workers' struggle against speed-up, against the division of labour and work organization, and against the rapid rate of attrition of labour-power, a direct consequence *of this process that goes all by itself.*

Thus if everything changes, if the concrete is that which changes, it is quite clear that a theory's pretension to possessing in itself, in advance, the whole truth of that which is changing and will continue to change is quite literally delusional and absurd. What is more, if the concrete is that which changes, it is not what one simply 'sees' changing that is the reason for change. This remark is of the greatest importance in the struggle against a false idea of Marxist theory. For there are Marxists who say: 'Granted: Marxist theory cannot claim to possess, in advance, the truth about its object, for, inasmuch as its object is by nature 'historical', it cannot know it in advance; it can know it only if it too submits to the *historical* character of its object, *by assigning itself, as theory, a historical character*, thus enabling theory not only not to betray its object by claiming to be, in advance, its absolute truth, but also, in averting this danger, truly to understand its object. So understood, Marxist theory can avert this danger only *by assigning itself* the preventive features of its object: historical features.[27] This is the interpretation of Marxist theory as *historicist* and of Marxism as an 'absolute historicism' to which Gramsci's name remains attached.[28]

2

The Absolute Empiricism
of Antonio Gramsci

The obvious advantage of the historicist conception of
Marxist theory is that it avoids the very serious danger
of conceiving of knowledge of the concrete as the simple
'application' of a philosophical 'theory' which is possessed
in advance of knowledge of the concrete, or the principle
of such knowledge. It is clear that, by explicitly referring
to Gramsci's thought and 'actively construing' it as an
'absolute historicism', the Italian Communist Party, under
Togliatti's lead,[1] very largely succeeded in steering clear of
a conception of the truth of the concrete as application
of an absolute theory, the defining feature, precisely, of
one of the forms of the Stalinist deviation in both theory
and also politics of the most 'concrete' kind. Without this
official recourse to Gramsci and the good fortune of being
able to refer to the thought of an Italian political leader
who, even before the war, during his prison years, proved
capable of struggling practically single-handed against
the tendencies of his own party's leadership in order to
propose a conception of Marxist theory that broke with
the dogmatism of truth and its 'application', there is no
understanding the Italian Communist Party's post-war

history or its profound originality in a world that was to
be dominated by Stalinist ideology and practices for a long
time to come. We may say that *historicism* is, in Gramsci,
an indeterminate form of anti-dogmatism.

I say 'an indeterminate form', because dogmatism
has several possible contraries, of which historicism is
only one. What is more, historicism is 'indeterminate'
in the sense that it is sound only by virtue of what it
rejects; it is weak as far as what it affirms is concerned.
I say this to bring out, alongside the ideological and
political merits of the historicist interpretation of Marxist
theory, its theoretical weak spot (hence also, possibly,
its ideological and political weak spot). For when one
says that the *concrete is always changing*, and when one
equates change with history in order to maintain that *the
concrete is historical*, historical through and through, one
falls back on a very impoverished idea of *history, which is
considered to be mere change*. It is not true that history is,
and is nothing but, change. There are, in history, relatively
stable structures that subsist for long periods beneath the
changes that affect them. We may even, going further,
maintain that these changes not only are changes *of* these
stable structures, but that they are produced *by* these stable
structures – not as their gratuitous expressions, but as so
many means of producing and reproducing their stability.

Thus Marx has shown that the capitalist mode of
production, the mode of production that continually
and ever more rapidly 'revolutionizes'[2] its productive
forces, the one that produces impressive, ever-increasing
speed, is intelligible only on the basis of *a relatively stable
structure, that of the capitalist relation of production*.[3]
We have, then, a paradox: this stable structure is antagonistic, it is the structure of the antagonism which divides
the classes into classes; yet it is this antagonism which
makes it possible to understand that all the changes in the
history of capitalist social formations – not in their details,
which, at the limit, may also be due to chance, but in their
essence – are so many means of perpetuating this stable
structure of the class relation of capitalist exploitation, the
stable structure of the conflictual division of all of society

into two basic classes, one of which possesses [*détient*] the means of production, while the other sells its labour-power. What is quite remarkable in the views that we owe to Marx is the idea that this antagonistic structure *cannot remain stable, remain the same, unless it produces change in its own antagonistic poles as the means of perpetuating its stability.*

Thus it is that there is a history of the capitalist mode of production.[4] This history is, above all, the history of the means and forms of exploitation and class struggle and, at the same time, the history of the transformation (change) of the classes that are party to the basic antagonistic relation. Thus it is that the bourgeoisie changes: once 'competitive', it becomes monopolistic and imperialist, and this brings with it, by a domino effect, a whole series of changes in the class fractions dependent on the bourgeoisie. Thus it is that the working class changes, transformed by the means of extracting, incessantly, more and more surplus value. Thus it is that, in the intermediate zones between the two antagonistic classes (in the urban and rural petty bourgeoisie), the boundary-lines shift: whole sections of the middle classes sink into the ranks of salaried workers [*le salariat*] or the working class. Thus it is that the bourgeoisie's class struggle alters strategies, means and forms as a function of the resistance of the workers' class struggle.

When we have arrived at this viewpoint, which is Marx's (and who has offered us a better one, one that effectively accounts for this set of phenomena?), we are no longer in historicism. We no longer define history as mere change or, a fortiori, as a change in viewpoints on history, and even less as the sum of the whole set of viewpoints on it. (What allows us, in accordance with the logic of historicism, to add them up and talk about their sum?) History is indeed defined by change, but as the condition and means, produced by a stable structure, of that stable structure's reproduction. Change accordingly appears as, simply, the very form by means of which the relatively stable structure (that of the mode of production) reproduces itself.

Under these conditions, to understand 'concrete' change 'concretely', we must *first* come to understand and define this stable structure, for only the conditions of its stability make it possible to understand change as that which allows this structure to perpetuate itself beneath, and in, and through, change itself.

Things are not all that complicated or hard to grasp. If the extortion of surplus value (the core of exploitation) takes place within a relationship of antagonistic class struggle, anyone can see that, to maintain this exploitation, hence to perpetuate the stability of the capitalist relation of production *in* the confrontation of class struggle, it is necessary to face the consequences of this confrontation: the forms of class struggle must change, and the classes party to it must therefore change as well. That is why there is a history of the capitalist mode of production, although the antagonistic structure of this mode of production remains relatively stable, remains the same, beneath the transformed forms of exploitation and class struggle, which never stop changing in order to perpetuate the stability of the mode of production.

It is well known that Marx sometimes speaks of the 'eternity' of a mode of production in order to give forceful expression to this stability.[5] It is, however, also well known that the same Marx who thus speaks of the 'eternity' of the capitalist mode of production never tires of pointing out the historical changes required or produced by the class struggle, whether it is a question of the history of the working day or the history of the transformation of labour-power (women and children, etc.). In the process, Marx discusses the 'concrete': he sketches a 'concrete analysis' of working conditions, the length of the working day, the reason for it, and the struggles to limit it, and he explains why the bourgeoisie itself ultimately *changed its strategy*, why it had the Ten Hour Bill voted through and, the better to exploit its workers, turned towards 'relative surplus value', in other words, the mechanization of production, which, by bringing a greater number of products onto the market at lower prices, made it possible to lower wages in the same, if not in greater proportion, and so on. Marx can sketch this 'concrete analysis' of these 'concrete' changes, however, only on condition that he relates them to the relatively stable structure that produces them as the condition for the perpetuation of its stability.

I mention only this argument, because I do not want to embark on a properly philosophical discussion of historicism, which embroils Marxism in absurd problems, such as that of knowing, since everything is historical, whether *the proposition 'everything is historical'* is also historical and, if so, what the word 'historical' might signify: if the only meaning it has is historical, we find ourselves going round in circles.[6] Put simply, this means that historicism reduces the whole of the real to the historical; only the historical exists. This reduces not just all knowledge, but also every signification and every word to the historical, which, consequently, no word is capable of explaining or even *saying*, since every word and every meaning are, in advance, historical. You are familiar with ordinary bicycles, which have two wheels: you pedal away and you get somewhere. There are bicycles in rehabilitation centres as well, but they have no wheels. You pedal away and you get nowhere. *Historicism is a bicycle with no wheels*. You can get on it and pedal away, but you stay right where you are. That is what happens when one proclaims that everything changes and that history is change and everything is history.

It must not be supposed that this philosophical interpretation of Marxism is without consequences. Every philosophy has binding consequences, theoretical, practical, ideological and, ultimately, political consequences, from the moment it ceases to be individual in order to inspire a political party's theory, practice and ideology – a fortiori when it is in order to be disseminated among the popular masses by the party and its actions. I do not at all mean to suggest by this that philosophy is the motor of history, even if it acts through the intermediary of a Communist party. It is always the broad masses who 'make history'.[7] Their experience is, however, collected, analysed and synthesized by the party, which, in the form of a political line, slogans and forms of action and organization, gives back to the masses what it has received from them. It is *in this moment* of the analysis and synthesis of experiences – very precisely, *in the moment of the analysis*, at the level of its leadership, of these experiences collectively gathered by the whole party – that philosophy intervenes: in the case to hand, the interpretation of Marxism that is given and received. It is in this very precise way that historicism can have theoretical and practical consequences.

Because everything is historical for historicism, it has a tendency to reduce all the really existing differences recognized in the Marxist tradition one to the other, so as to find itself, in the final analysis, facing 'history' alone. This can be seen very clearly in Gramsci, who has a tendency to reduce Marxist theory ('historical materialism') to philosophy, philosophy to politics, and politics to history.[8] By means of this series of successive reductions, which tend to obliterate recognized, important differences, Marxism is reduced, not really to history (which is real), but to a philosophy of history, to a philosophy of the historical as the sole truth of all differences, that is, to 'absolute historicism'. Very important, and symptomatic, consequences obviously follow.

For example, historical materialism tends to be 'obliterated' in Gramsci – obliterated, that is to say, reduced to Marxist philosophy, termed 'the philosophy of praxis'. This obviously does not mean that Gramsci jettisons historical materialism in its entirety, but, for example – this is very instructive – it means that he manifestly does not have a very precise idea of what a theory of the 'infrastructure' might be; a smattering of references aside, the infrastructure is practically absent from his writings. If the infrastructure disappears, what is left is the 'superstructure'; it is no accident that Gramsci is the first theorist to have taken a real interest in the phenomena of the superstructure, the state and the ideologies. However, if the superstructure alone remains on stage, while the infrastructure is banished to the wings, the organic ties that explain the existence and function of the superstructure in its relations to the infrastructure – which explain that the superstructure plays a decisive role in the reproduction of the infrastructure, hence in the reproduction of the relation of production – are not truly taken into consideration and thought in their full reality.

Thus the superstructure leads a ghostly existence in Gramsci: *there is* the state, *there is* law, *there are* the ideologies, that's just the way it is. We know nothing, or next to nothing, about why *there is* superstructure [*pourquoi il y a de la superstructure*]. All one can do with this superstructure is describe it and analyse its functioning at the very level of its manifestation, as if it were not commanded by the hidden bonds that tie it to the infrastructure.

This is, moreover, the reason that, when Gramsci does discuss it, he plainly does not like this distinction between infrastructure and superstructure.[9] He says that in so many words. He considers it to be a mechanistic and 'metaphysical' distinction, that is, one that artificially separates realities that are not separate. In his critique of Bukharin's mechanistic *Manual*,[10] he has no trouble criticizing this distinction as mechanistic:[11] nothing is easier to do. In the process, however, in taking the *Manual*'s crude distortions as a pretext, he does what, at heart, he wants to do: he can throw the baby out with the bathwater, he can dismiss the distinction between infrastructure and superstructure, which does not suit him, by dismissing Bukharin's mechanistic interpretations. Once he has rid himself of this distinction, Gramsci can abandon himself to the delights of the superstructure – all by itself.

No wonder, then, that this superstructure leads a ghostly existence in Gramsci. It was absolutely crucial to have put the accent on the importance of the superstructure, and to have suggested (albeit timidly) that the superstructure penetrates the infrastructure. The unity of this 'penetration', however, while it is described, is not truly thought and, what is more, this penetration itself is thought *from the point of view of the superstructure*; we do not really learn *what other thing* this superstructure penetrates. In a period in which the Stalinian political line was being carried out in the name of the 'development of the productive forces', understood as instruments and means of production, while man was simultaneously declared to be 'the most valuable capital (!)' (economism = humanism),[12] hence an element of the infrastructure, it was crucial to have insisted on the superstructure, the role of the state and, above all, politics, a politics at antipodes from Stalin's. There was, in this, the means with which to found a critique of economism, which Gramsci unerringly identified with Stalin's theoretical and political deviation – and thus the means with which to open up new paths for the workers' movement. But ...

But this superstructure, which it is Gramsci's historical and political merit to have thus highlighted as the main issue to oppose to Stalinian economism, leads, it must be said, a singular existence in Gramsci's theoretical universe. In fact, from the moment the infrastructure is neglected, the superstructure remains very much alone – alone with itself. As nothing that has been truly thought attaches this superstructure to an evanescent infrastructure, Gramsci finds himself obliged to think it *by itself*. And to think something by itself is to *describe* it; it is to look, with greater or lesser success, but randomly, for interconnections and points of comparison between the elements described. Look! *There is* the state, *there is* law, *there are* ideologies. Why are they there? A mystery. What are they made of? Of such-and-such elements. What relationships can we observe and describe between these realities? This or that relationship. Why these particular relationships? A mystery. *That is how things are*, full-stop. The task is to describe them and to try to understand them by setting out from a description of them, from an enumeration, and by enumerating and comparing their elements. Thus historicism is a form of empiricism. This appears quite clearly in Gramsci.

It appears, for example, in the circumstance that Gramsci, who insists so heavily on the superstructure, fails to provide even the beginnings of a theory of the ideologies. He contents himself with saying that ideology is a social 'cement'. That does not go very far. And he contents himself with repeating the famous sentence from Marx's Preface (1859)[13] which has it that 'it is in ideology that men become conscious of their struggle and fight it out',[14] a highly debatable sentence. In the case of ideology, plainly, empiricism produces nothing. That's just how it is. The same thing appears, the other way around, in the case of the intellectuals. Here, Gramsci is able to draw a connection between observed elements that makes eminently good sense. He does not content himself with repeating what Marx has already said; he thinks what Marx said, and he says new things: that intellectuals are usually 'organic', are, that is, a given society's intellectuals; that the function of intellectuals is not, as is all too often supposed, to think for thought's sake, but to organize, and serve as the self-consciousness of, a culture that they disseminate among the masses; that the types of intellectuals vary with the forms of societies, and so on.[15] These are very rich notions. At the same time, however, they are notions that seem to stand isolated, in their ensemble, in the chequered field of Gramsci's thought: as if, here, by a happy accident, empiricism had produced a felicitous result, contrary to the case of the ideologies.

Notions standing isolated in a body of thought? Not exactly; for the idea of the 'intellectuals' that Gramsci arrives at depends on another idea, deeply rooted in him, about the *normal type of historical unity* that every authentic historical 'epoch' should in his view display. It is quite as if history, for Gramsci, *truly* comes about only when it attains the state of a 'beautiful totality', not so much when a mode of production reaches its apogee, as when a genuine 'historical bloc' is constituted, one capable of uniting all men in the unity of a practice and an ethics – in short, of a culture.

That is why the role of the 'organic intellectuals' is so important for Gramsci, and it is also why he 'discovered' their existence. For this unity of a culture comes about only when the culture does not remain the property of the 'intellectuals', but penetrates the immense mass of 'simple souls', the people. And this extension is only possible when the dominant values, those of the culture of the 'great', are capable of getting themselves received, accepted and acknowledged by the 'simple souls'. This does not always happen. When it fails to happen, we do not have to do with an *authentic* 'historical epoch', a *true* 'historical bloc' capable of ensuring its hegemony, of dominating by convincing, through persuasion and through the popularization of its own ideas among the people. When it happens, we have to do with a true 'historical epoch', a 'historical bloc' that is *normal*, that is *as it ought to be*; and, in that case, the class in power can dominate the people by persuading it, by obtaining its accord, its free consent, by bringing it freely to accept the dominant class's ideas and its own exploitation, hence its oppression.

This is where the 'organic intellectuals' step in. For this establishment of hegemony, of a domination freely accepted by the dominated, this dissemination of the dominant ideas among all the people, is impossible without what Gramsci calls *the educational role of the state*. If these ideas and values are to be freely accepted by the people, they must be taught to it in forms suited to its intelligence. The dominant class and the people therefore need educators, schoolmasters in the strong sense of the word, to teach the people the ideas that seal the unity of the 'historical bloc' under the dominant class, to see to it that these ideas penetrate the people, and even to inflict a certain violence on the people (every act of education presupposes a certain violence) so that it allows itself to be formed and fashioned by these ideas. This is the task of the 'organic intellectuals', on condition, of course, that we do not suppose that the 'values' cementing the 'historical bloc' are reducible to ideas. It is a question of an ensemble of practices, from the practices of production to political, moral and religious practices. It is a veritable *concrete universal ethics*.

Everyone knows the example from which Gramsci draws his reflections on the organic intellectuals. Paradoxically, *it is the Church*.[16] He carefully analyses the recruitment of the Church's 'intellectuals' (first and foremost, among the poor peasantry, for whom becoming a priest spells social advancement), the Church's abiding concern to avoid, at all costs, the emergence of a rift between the 'intellectuals' and the 'simple souls', the creation of monastic orders to forestall such a rift, and so on. It is an astonishing example, for the Church is not, after all, a 'historical bloc'; it is an ideological apparatus that is always, more or less, a *state* apparatus.

Gramsci, however, extends his reflections on the Church with comparative reflections on the history of France and Italy, contrasting France – which, in the Revolution, successfully constituted a 'historical bloc', endowing itself with an *authentic educator state* and forming an integral corps of organic intellectuals to take all the tasks of hegemony in hand – with Italy, which proved unable to carry out its bourgeois revolution, hence to found an *authentic* 'historical bloc' and, consequently, to endow itself with a *true* corps of organic intellectuals.[17] Everyone knows Gramsci's laments over Italian intellectuals, foreign to their nation from the Renaissance on, ready to peddle their services to the highest foreign bidder in order to pursue brilliant careers abroad, political or of some other kind. When a state does not succeed in bringing about an authentic universal ethical unity in its people, it has no use for its intellectuals, who, moreover, are no longer *its* intellectuals, and who draw the appropriate conclusion by becoming 'cosmopolitan intellectuals': they leave to serve foreign masters.

When we reflect, even as schematically as we are doing here, on the unity of all these themes in Gramsci (more often than not, they are themes rather than concepts), we notice several surprising things.

We discover, first of all, that Gramsci not only neglects the infrastructure in order to discuss the superstructure alone, but, further, that he tends to replace the Marxist concept *mode of production* with the concept *'historical bloc'*. This is obviously in keeping with the logic of his historicism, if it is true that the mode of production is defined by a relatively *stable* social-material relation, the relation of production, in which the two basic classes' antagonism plays itself out, whereas the 'historical bloc' evokes something altogether different: the mere *event* of an ethical historical unity, which is clearly historical from end to end, in that it may be realized (France) or not (Italy).

Reducing the Marxist concept 'mode of production' to the advantage of the concept 'historical bloc' thus *realizes* historicism's underlying tendency: everything is history, everything changes, and the ideal form of unity may or may not come about. It is a matter of history: one observes the facts, and if one seeks the causes, one is cast into history's infinity, with no fixed point.

One then discovers, however, that it is no accident that Gramsci sets out from the Church and ends up in France and Italy, since he finds his concept 'organic intellectuals' in the Church and its history. To which 'sphere' does the Church belong, after all, if not to that of the ideologies, the ideological apparatuses that can be state apparatuses (the Church well and truly was one), and therefore *to the superstructure*? Where did Gramsci find his model of a perfect, universal ethical unity, if not in the Catholic (universal) Church, which succeeded so well in never cutting itself off from the 'simple souls', taking the greatest possible pains, rather, to put the best of its organic intellectuals to work instilling its truths in them, preaching them to them, teaching them to them, educating them in the love of God and submission to the Church? ... That all this happens in ideology and, therefore, in all the gestures and choices of practical life (once we have learnt that ideology is not 'ideas'), is more than clear.

What is not just surprising but astounding, however, is that Gramsci, who describes the Church's politics so well, nowhere sketches out a *theory of the Church* (to say nothing of religion, Marxist thought's grey area).[18] The reason is that he has no theory of the ideologies – not because he takes no interest in them, but because his historicism bars him from asking the question by depriving him of the means of asking it (from the moment he neglects the infrastructure). What is astounding is the reason for which Gramsci turns to the Church to look not for an example, but for the very *essence*, the *realized* essence, of the 'beautiful ethical totality' that he goes on to project onto the state of the 'historical bloc'. The reason is that he discovers a profound identity between the unity of an ideological state apparatus and the unity of the ethical state; *it is the ideological unity of the Church, ensured by its 'organic intellectuals', which gives him the theoretical key to the unity of the ethical state.* The upshot is that he thinks the state itself by setting out from ideology. Here we have another 'historicist' reduction.

For, to conclude, what is striking in Gramsci is, notably, this conception of the state of the ideal 'historical bloc', conceived of as an *ethical totality* unified by the hegemony it exercises over 'the people' through its 'organic intellectuals'. This universal consensus is ensured by the educational activity of the state and its intellectuals, which does not unfold without a certain violence; it is inflicted on men in order to inculcate ideas and practices in them that will prompt a profound ethical transformation in them, turning them into 'citizens' of this ethical state.

We would look in vain, in this ideal figure (I mean, of course, at this level of abstraction), for vestiges of the classes and the class struggle. Not only is the infrastructure neglected, not only is everything practically reduced to the superstructure, but, in the superstructure, the state is reduced to ideology; rather, since Gramsci does not like to talk about ideology in connection with the state, the state is reduced to this *ethical unity* on the one hand and, on the other, to the fact that this unity is at once imposed and consented to. In other words, it is reduced to what Gramsci calls 'hegemony'.

We can only conclude that 'absolute' historicism, which is philosophically *unthinkable*, here confesses its own philosophical impotence by *exhibiting*, in a different domain, with regard to the Church, the state, and so on, the philosophical thinking that subtends it: *normative* and, consequently, idealist thinking. Just as there exists, for Gramsci, the 'model' of the Church, so there exists, for him, the 'model' of France, both of them perfect and successful in their kind and homogeneous with each other. There exists, as well, the 'counter-model' of Italy, that *abnormal* country which, *abnormally*, has not even managed to become a nation, to make 'its French Revolution' and endow itself with an authentic state. In short, there exist, in history, the normal and the pathological. Why? Gramsci naturally refers us to history, that is,[19] the infinity of historical facts, without _____, without modes of production, without class struggles (not entirely: _____ a communist), with neither a material state nor ideological state apparatuses: ad infinitum, historical facts _____ stable making it possible to think change, _____ fact.

And, the height of paradox: when this historicist yet normative thought finds itself confronted with _____ which corresponds neither to its ideal _____ nor to the ideal conditions of its _____ *of a real state nonetheless, one that realizes the unity* _____ economic, political and 'moral' reforms, and which likewise educates the _____ of a state that is well and truly functional, but is not _____ of a 'French revolution' (for instance, the Italian state), Gramsci speaks of a '*passive* revolution'.[20]

This means that, in this case, history was not made *as it* _____. Rather than coming from below, from a unifying popular movement, the revolution came from above; it was made in _____ by the bourgeoisie allied with the monarchy, and the people remained _____ in it. It is not at all certain that the people was _____ here; simply, the course of history, however historical it may _____, was not *what it ought to have been*. This means that there is history and history, good historicity and bad. With that, historicism splits in two; yet the two parts of _____ subsumed under a single norm, which _____ them, it is unclear why, unless one thinks in _____.

This concept of 'passive revolution' receives an immense extension in Gramsci. He does not employ it solely in order to think the _____ of the popular Risorgimento and the usurpation of its historical tasks by the alliance concluded between Cavour and the monarchy.[21] He employs it for fascism and Nazism[22] as well; finally, he employs it, between the lines, for Stalin's USSR. It is true that he 'gets at' something that is quite accurate with this designation: at the fact that popular initiative is absent from these singular 'revolutions'; that everything in them comes from above; that, consequently, division holds sway between the state, which grows increasingly more powerful and more arbitrary, and the popular masses, who are increasingly 'strangers' to their historical destiny; and that, rather than the reign of the beautiful unity of an ethical state, we see the state penetrate the masses and 'civil society' from without, in order to impose its reforms on them and organize people in the forced, artificial unity of state trade unions and the party of the state. And, because the 'passive', abnormal revolution must always be contrasted to an active, normal revolution, Gramsci is not far from opposing, to all these states that are non-ethical and non-universal in their unity, the image of another sort of revolution, which, for its part, is active and therefore normal, a revolution unfolding at the same time beyond the seas, in Roosevelt's America: the revolution of the New Deal.

There is no denying that, with this terminology and these examples, Gramsci gets at something in the real [*quelque chose de la réalité*]. The question, however, is *what* he gets at, and *how*. We cannot refrain from making two remarks about this.

First, we may note that Gramsci almost never uses a term which is, of course, open to criticism, yet has, notwithstanding, been consecrated by its use in Marxist theory: the term *counter-revolution*. In the same vein, we may note that Gramsci, who thinks the course of history in terms of active and passive 'revolutions', would appear to be insensitive to the phenomena of *regression*, or even of *lag* or *stagnation*. These two remarks both tend in the same direction: for Gramsci, who thinks within a good old idealist philosophy of history, the course of history is oriented in advance: history has a direction, hence a goal. His whole critique of Bukharin's *Manual* has clearly distanced him from mechanism, but only to bring him closer to teleology. There is a striking indication of this: it is the reason that Gramsci *constantly harks back* to two absurd (because idealist) sentences of Marx's in the Preface to the *Contribution*:[23] 'A mode of production never disappears before it has exhausted all the resources of its productive forces' and 'humanity sets itself only such tasks as it is able to accomplish'.[24] In these two sentences, which *literally mean nothing*, and whose occurrence in Marx is explained only by the survival of a philosophy of history, Gramsci detects the touchstone and theoretical foundation of Marx's thinking on history!

We can understand, then, why Gramsci thinks all history within a single category, the category of revolution, and why, in his normative perspective, he has no other recourse than to think history *either* in the form of the active revolution that bears within itself the premises and the promise of an authentic ethical state, *or* in that of the 'passive revolution' that is carried out under a bad, non-ethical state and fails to produce authentic cultural unity among its citizens.

However, this notion of 'passive revolution', which, of course, simultaneously evokes the accompanying notion of active revolution (an expression that Gramsci does not use as such), reveals that, for Gramsci, the essence of history, through the normal or abnormal forms of revolution, is *activity*: either the presence of activity or the absence of activity. To be sure, it is, in the last resort, a question of the popular masses' activity (or non-activity), and this confers its progressive or even populist aspect on Gramsci's thought. The fact remains that it is plainly a question of activity.

To express, at this level of immediacy, which is to say, of abstraction, the 'essence' of history, Marx never speaks of *activity*, except in his early texts of critical Fichtean inspiration, and in the empiricist-materialist philosophy of history that he defends in *The German Ideology*. If, again *at this level*, we had to identify the term that Marx considers apt to designate the 'essence' of history, it would, without a doubt, be *practice*. Activity, however, which so interests Gramsci, stands to practice as *its internal truth*. Activity lies concealed in every practice. Whose activity? That of individuals, of 'men', obviously. That is why the idealism of activity refers us quite naturally and directly to the idealism of the 'men who make history',[25] to the idealism of the activity of individuals, whom we see 'starting out from themselves' in *The German Ideology*,[26] whom we see acting, acting in every sense of the term, producing consumer goods, acting in politics, ethics, and so on. In these conditions, we will not be surprised to find the major them of *humanism* in Gramsci, as well as an explicit affirmation of the identity between '*absolute historicism*' and '*absolute humanism*'.[27] We must grant Gramsci, if not the merit of thinking correctly, at least that of thinking consistently what he thinks wrong. That is something of great value for those who know how to read.

We may, however, make another remark about, again, this 'passive revolution' and the consequences of the introduction of this concept as an essential concept in Gramsci's view. If Gramsci 'gets at' something real [*quelque chose du réel*], *how* does he do so? The biggest disappointment lies in store for us here. For Gramsci proffers, under cover of a normative philosophy of history, nothing but pure, *superficial descriptions*. Let us be clear: we should not disdain the superficial, which can contain certain elements of knowledge and, above all, hints and symptoms that we can bring to the threshold of real knowledge, on condition that we carry out a genuine analysis of them. Yet, as it presents itself, the superficial is superficial. What do we gain by observing that there are revolutions that come from the popular masses and others that, paradoxically, are made by the dominant class? What – unless we need to unify all history in advance under the concept of revolution – authorizes the play on words that consists in using the word 'revolution' for, at the same time, the French Revolution, Roosevelt, Cavour, Mussolini and Hitler, and Stalin? In what way does the use of the term 'revolution' in the expression 'passive revolution' provide us with the least knowledge? Does the unwarranted use of this term not, rather, plunge us into confusion? And what do we gain by *describing*, as Gramsci does, the general characteristics of 'passive revolution' as opposed to active or authentic revolution?

To be sure, we do learn certain things. We learn, above all, that the dominant class can accomplish tasks that, *normally, should have* been accomplished by the popular masses. A lot of good that does us! Who can say that *the same tasks* would have been involved if the popular movement had existed? That can be affirmed only by virtue of a teleological conception of history, one that establishes the tasks, the same tasks, in advance. If the popular masses accomplish them, so much the better. If, however, they are incapable of doing so, then the dominant class will accomplish them, and that is 'not good', because things will sooner or later go awry. ...

And, to broach the most ticklish point in this pseudo-theory of history: How does Gramsci explain the fact that, when certain tasks are historically on history's 'agenda' (establishing a national state, carrying out a revolution, and so on), the popular masses can sometimes be present and sometimes be absent? How does he explain the fact that, when certain tasks are historically on history's agenda and the popular masses do not turn out to perform them, it just so happens (what a coincidence!) that the dominant classes are on hand to accomplish them, where, for centuries, *no one* happened to be on hand to perform them (the case of Italy itself)?

Gramsci, or a Gramscian philosopher, could always reply by citing a series of *historical* facts, but since they will be just as superficial, because just as empirical, as the fact to be explained, he will never be able to get the better of the difficulty that he himself has artificially created in setting out from his philosophy. For no more than we can explain the water in this glass with reference to all the waterways in the world can we explain a historical fact (in the sense of an immediate historical fact) by the succession, however long and multifaceted it may be, of all the historical facts in the world. That is why, even in what is novel about them, Gramsci's 'analyses' – *which are not analyses*, but the *description* of a historical given, the breakdown of this given into certain elements that are arbitrarily singled out, and the comparison of these elements with other elements drawn from other historical givens – do not produce real knowledge, but illusions of knowledge, naturally with the 'positive' aspect contained by all illusions, which are not errors.

The reason for this is quite clear. Since Gramsci is self-consistent, and since he has divulged his philosophical 'self-consciousness' with his declaration of 'absolute historicism', he has a natural tendency to suppose that the immediate historical given is, as such, its own illumination, its own truth. That is why he confines himself strictly to the historical given, never going beyond its limits. That is why he contents himself with describing it and withdrawing from the elements that he arbitrarily 'abstracts' from it, compared with other elements (just as arbitrarily) extracted from other historical givens, *the internal truth* of this historical given, which thus illuminates itself with its own light. 'If the essence of things were immediately visible', Marx writes, 'there would be no need for science.'[28]

For Gramsci, the essence of the historical (and everything is historical) is immediately visible, at the price of a few empirical abstractions and a few empirical comparisons. Spinoza said that the concept 'dog' does not bark.[29] Let us take a 'historical' example that would have been dear to Gramsci, and talk about the geese of the Capitol. We could make Gramsci confess that the concept 'goose' does not cackle not because it is a concept, but because the concept does not exist. He could say that the concept 'history' is not historical not because history is not historical (it is nothing but that), but because there is no concept 'history'. In truth, if there is no concept 'history', we already know why: there is, in Gramsci, an Idea of history, or, again, history is the Idea, that is, it pursues an End.

If the historical contains its own essence in itself, immediately (that is to say, empirically), it suffices, at the limit, to attend to the succession of historical events as they present themselves, in their empiricity. That is just what Gramsci does, taking arbitrary descriptions for authentic analyses. *Gramsci is not a theorist of history, but a reader of history*: history, for him, resembles a text that immediately divulges its meaning to the one who reads it. Its meaning. ... Exactly. The whole illusion is there. For a text delivers up, not *its* meaning to the one who reads it, but *a* meaning, born of the encounter of the imposition or emergence of a meaning in the text with all the other texts that fill or haunt its reader's mind because they are 'in the air'. This amounts to saying that Gramsci 'reads' history in *the illusion* of absolute empiricism (identical with absolute historicism), which clings to the belief, for reasons having nothing to do with history, which it isolates in order to read it, that the meaning of history emerges directly from a reading of it.

It is here that things could be turned around, here that we should ask *the true question*: Why did Gramsci dwell in this illusion? Still better: *Why did he need this illusion?* Answering this question would plunge us into a lengthy investigation of the history of class struggles in Italy and the philosophical and political education of Italian intellectuals, of whom Gramsci, for all his singularity, is but a particular historical instance.

That, however, would obviously be to conceive of history very differently from the way Gramsci does. It would be to suggest the reasons that he so deftly dispenses himself of the obligation to discuss the infrastructure and, above all, to take it into account, or the mode and the relation of production, reproduction and even class struggle, or to broach anything that might resemble a theoretical analysis in the 'region' in which he has taken refuge: namely, the superstructure and, in the superstructure, politics.

For that, finally, is what everything comes down to: Gramsci is a politician [*un politique*], and a great politician. The leader of the Turin workers' councils, the great Leninist of the struggles of the early 1920s, the founder, with Togliatti, of the Italian Communist Party, the dogged adversary of Fascism, which held him prisoner until his death, the politically lucid critic of the theoretical dogmatism of an economistic tradition that, beginning with Bukharin, was to culminate in Stalin, the man who was able to embark, in opposition to his own party, on a battle against the CPSU's and the Komintern's politics from the depths of his prison – this man was an exceptional politician, and all those who knew him have extolled his intelligence, his force of character, and his impact on others in discussion and action.

Nothing is more natural, it will be said, than that a man so thoroughly steeped in politics should, in his theoretical writings, concern himself with politics. And the fact is that we need only read the *Prison Notebooks* to see that what Gramsci discusses in them is, first and foremost, politics. We must, however, go infinitely further. For to concern oneself with politics is one thing; it is quite another to uphold the philosophical thesis that 'everything is political'. I am talking about philosophy and, in talking about philosophy, I am *still* talking about the one to which Gramsci explicitly adheres, namely, the philosophy of absolute historicism, identical to absolute humanism.

How are we to understand these new developments? But the last word has yet to be said; only now does Gramsci utter it. To hear it, however, a bit of attention is required.

Gramsci refers to Marxism as 'the philosophy of praxis'. In so doing, he negates a traditional distinction that has, of course, been exploited and travestied, yet is not without its raison d'être: the distinction between 'historical materialism', or the principles of knowledge of the conditions and forms of the class struggle, and (so as not to use the despicable term 'dialectical materialism') 'Marxist philosophy'. Even if the term 'Marxist philosophy', which I do not endorse, must be replaced, there are reasons for this distinction, which can be defended.[30] Gramsci, however, rejects it; and he does so in order to integrate 'historical materialism' into the 'philosophy of praxis'. For him, they are the same thing. To put it plainly, in Gramsci's view, as in that of Mach, whom he has read and approved – the Mach whom Lenin so vehemently criticizes[31] – there is no difference between a piece of knowledge of a scientific character and a philosophical thesis: the former is reducible, in its essence, to the latter. *Thus everything is philosophical* (the sciences, religion, the arts, politics and so on). And the 'philosophy of practice' is the one philosophy in the world that has become conscious of the fact that everything is philosophy and that everyone is a philosopher.[32] If this is, at bottom, how things are, if everything *is* philosophy and has been from all eternity, what can philosophical activity possibly consist in? It can only

be a simple *critique* of false ideas about what exists, about
the sciences, politics, the arts, religion and so on, a critique
which, by exposing what is false, will reveal to people the
truth that they carry deep within themselves unawares.
This first and last truth is that *everything is philosophy*.

Everyone will recognize, in this idea of 'critique', the
old idealist notion that presupposes the existence of the
true and the power of the truth, which has the capacity, de
jure, to free itself from error, if only ordinary consciousness
(that of the 'simple souls') recognizes the light of the Truth
that dwells in the consciousness of the intellectuals. The
philosopher, unaware that he is one, can be one only because
there exist philosophers who know that they are philosophers, and know that everyone else is a philosopher without
knowing it, and know that everything is philosophy. An old
form of idealism, bound up with the theme of education (by
the state, by the party) so dear to Gramsci.

That the Truth dwells in all people without their
knowledge is one thing. What is surprising in Gramsci's
case, however, is that this philosophical Truth that dwells
in every human being is stated as follows: everything
is philosophy. The mystery resides here, but so does
its solution; for Gramsci, when he talks about Marx
and philosophy (Marxist philosophy is the only true
philosophy, the only one to dwell in the depths of all
philosophies, unbeknownst to them), does not just talk
about philosophy: he talks about 'the philosophy *of
praxis*'. The idea that this term merely served Gramsci
to camouflage his ideas in order to elude the censorship
of his gaolers, whom the name Marx or the adjective
Marxist would have put on the alert, is not taken seriously
by anyone today. The term philosophy of praxis unques-
tionably expresses Gramsci's own thinking. 'Praxis':
Gramsci, who could have used the Italian word *pratica*,
as we would say *philosophie de la pratique* [philosophy of
practice], borrowed the term praxis from Marx's 'Theses
on Feuerbach', in which the phrase 'philosophy of praxis'
does not occur, although 'philosophy' and 'praxis' do,
separately.[33] Is this an insignificant nuance? I do not think
so; for, by refusing to use the term practice – which can

be used by itself (practice), but can also be very readily modified and often is (political practice, social practice, aesthetic, philosophical, religious practice) – and by giving preference to the term praxis, Gramsci puts the accent, like Marx in the 'Theses on Feuerbach', where he speaks of the 'subjectivity' of 'praxis', on what is internal to all practice: namely, *activity*, as we already know.[34]

This philosophical predilection for the theme of activity, which is one of the themes that can be associated with the term praxis, is not at all devoid of meaning in Gramsci's thought. If everything is philosophy, and if activity constitutes the essence of philosophy, then this seemingly mysterious proposition, 'the philosophy of praxis', takes on a precise meaning. The philosophy of praxis is right to uphold the thesis that everything is philosophy if the essence of philosophy is in fact *activity*. We would here be very close to a philosophy of a Fichtean cast (in the beginning is the act) if we were not in historicist empiricism, as we are not in Fichte's transcendentalism. '*Everything is activity*' designates neither the transcendental a priori activity of the Act (Fichte) nor the concrete transcendental activity of the 'praxis' that *repeats*, in every predicative praxis, the *passive* synthesis of a pre-predicative praxis. (At the end of his life, Husserl too developed, in *Erfahrung und Urteil*,[35] a 'philosophy of praxis', but a concrete-constitutive one.) Rather, 'everything is activity' very simply and very mundanely designates *the empirical fact* that 'men', in other words, concrete individuals, are naturally – it's enough to take a look at them – and by essence 'active', be it in solitude or (and par excellence) in social life; and that it is their activity which 'makes history'.

Let us recapitulate. Everything is philosophy. The truth of every philosophy is the 'philosophy of praxis'. Praxis is, in its essence, activity. Therefore everything is activity. This thesis doubtless holds for the whole universe. Gramsci does not delve into that idea, but neither does he rule it out. In any case, *everything is activity* in the human world. This means that individuals are active and that it is their activity which makes history.

Here is the final point: if individuals are active, and it is evident that they are, it is also evident that they have different activities. There does not appear to be much in common between the activity of producing means of consumption and the activity of praying to God, or the activity of philosophizing, or political activity, or the activity of playing football. You might think so, but you're wrong: there exists an essence common to all these activities. More exactly, there is, *among these different activities*, one activity that is the essence of the others and, at the same time, *its own essence*: namely, politics. After saying that everything is philosophy, Gramsci declares that *every philosophy is political*.[36] Since we know that the essence of every philosophy is activity, we can confer a precise meaning on the word politics: *political activity*.[37] All this holds together extremely well.

Here, Gramsci is in his element, truly in his element, at the Archimedean point of every possible truth and every possible action, including every political action; and when Gramsci thinks political action, he means, beyond the shadow of a doubt, and par excellence, the revolutionary political action of the masses that the 'modern Prince', the communist party, guides toward the capture of state power.

The whole of this immense detour of thought, whose stages we have schematically marked off in order to arrive here, at this precise point, toward which the great political leader, between the walls of a squalid prison, leads the philosopher by the hand: all the way to the truth of all truths, the one that will enable the popular masses, if only they can read his handwritten notes some day and steep themselves in their truth, not to lift up the world,[38] but to 'change' it: to make the revolution at last.[39] The fact that this was thought in personal and political isolation, in the years in which, although the Popular Fronts were still standing, fascism was triumphing throughout the world, from the East to the West, and there was not a single ray of hope to brighten the future of the workers' movement, while nothing more could really come from the USSR, imprisoned in Stalinism – thus the fact that it was thought in the darkest, most desolate night in modern history – cannot but seize readers with emotion and make them tremble in admiration, still full of illusions as we are about our own future today.

That, however, does not dispense us from the obligation to subject Gramsci's ideas on politics to close examination – not for the philosophical pleasure of assessing them (appreciating their value or appraising their errors), but because these ideas have in fact, as their author wished, penetrated broad masses throughout the world, not just in Italy, where, since Togliatti, Gramsci has been treated as the Italian Communist Party's official theorist and has also been very widely adopted well beyond the Party and the left-wing trade unions, but also because his thought is on its way to becoming hegemonic in communist circles and their peripheries in Spain, England, Japan, the United States, and many other capitalist countries. The fact is that Gramsci's thought is on its way to becoming the acknowledged thought of what is known as Eurocommunism. It is on those grounds that I would here like to examine the Gramscian themes involving politics: for political reasons. It is these reasons alone that have obliged me to make the long detour that precedes, so that we can gain a clear view of the place where everything is decided: politics.

To understand Gramsci's idea of politics, however, we have to make one more detour. To begin with, we need to be aware that Gramsci thinks in *so original a way that one wonders to what extent he can still be associated with Marx.* For instance, we have seen that Gramsci did not really take into account, or even neglected (and, possibly, was ignorant of on certain points, because he did not have access to *Capital* in prison?) the Marxist theory of the 'mode of production', the infrastructure and the relation of production. To this list of things neglected, we must add that which, together with the theory of the relation of production, commands everything, especially the whole Marxist theory of the superstructure (although Marx never explicitly pronounced on this point): the theory of *reproduction*.

This set of concepts is to be found in black and white in Marx. Some are developed at great length (the infrastructure, the capitalist relation of production, and reproduction – the last of these concepts is, admittedly, developed only with respect to the reproduction of constant capital and labour-power); the others are developed more briefly (the mode of production, the superstructure and all its 'elements': the state, law and the ideologies).

Once all these decisive ideas are neglected or abandoned, however, and once it is shown that something (which is, moreover, poorly delimited) of the superstructure penetrates the infrastructure – this is the outline of a demonstration that we can 'read' the infrastructure setting out from the superstructure, and thus of an invitation to carry out this 'reading' – Gramsci *constructs, in his way, at a far remove from Marx*, his own theory.

Instead of the distinction between infrastructure and superstructure, which he criticizes as mechanistic and metaphysical, Gramsci presents us with a different distinction, apparently an old acquaintance: that *between the state* and *civil society*.[40] I say 'apparently', because, in the bourgeois idealist philosophical, economic and political tradition, this distinction figures explicitly from the seventeenth century on. Hegel registers it in his philosophy of right, and precisely defines it, stipulating that the state is the realization of the Idea, hence of the concrete universal, and that civil society is the 'system of needs', *private* needs, that is, the needs of work and economic production and consumption, but that it *contains apparatuses* (the courts, the police) as well as 'civil' *organizations* (the corporations).[41] In fact, Gramsci does not take this old distinction over term for term: he assigns 'civil society' a new meaning. Thinking within the bourgeois legal distinction public/private, he presents civil society as the whole set of private associations existing outside the state. The state is public; they are private. Gramsci puts the Churches, the school system, the political parties, the trade unions and so on among their number.[42]

What stands out is their private nature. Thus they are not public; thus they have no de jure relationship with the state. At the same time, however, Gramsci describes these associations as 'hegemonic apparatuses', borrowing the term apparatus from the Marxist theory of the state and the term hegemony from the Leninist tradition. We are never told anything more about these 'hegemonic apparatuses', about the differences between them, about their structure, or about the motor of their functioning. We know only that they are 'apparatuses'. However, this term, which served Marx and Lenin as a provisional 'solution' when they discussed the state, is not explained. We also know that they are 'hegemonic', that is, that they produce a consensus effect in the popular masses. In very Aristotelian fashion, Gramsci, declaring that these apparatuses are 'hegemonic', defines them by the end they pursue, which is identical to the effect they produce. Otherwise, they would not be what they are.

When someone says 'an umbrella is when it rains', people laugh. But when someone says 'an umbrella protects you from the rain', they don't laugh, and that is a shame, for we learn nothing about the umbrella. The question of the cause of the hegemonic in the hegemonic apparatuses is left hanging; Gramsci never tells us anything about that. To say that 'hegemony is when people say yes' does not get us very far. One can say yes because one freely consents; one can say yes under duress. Rousseau knew this when he wrote about the robber who brings you to say yes by pointing a revolver at your nose.[43] To put it plainly: force too can be a means of hegemony. And force can be exercised in several different ways, either by physical violence, or by the threat embodied by its presence, but without violence (Lyautey's policy: showing one's force in order not to have to use it, not showing one's force in order to use it), or, again – a more subtle method – by its absence. (The troops responsible for maintaining order consigned to their barracks, the tanks under the trees of the Forest of Rambouillet:[44] everyone knows that they exist and would intervene if … Order reigns, therefore, thanks to their very absence, just as, by its absence, an invisible, non-circulating stock of gold and securities maintains the requisite order on the market for capital, currencies and securities.[45]) In short, one says nothing about hegemony when one does not say *how* it is maintained and *how* it gains acceptance. One remains at the level of description.

If I insist on this notion, it is because it will serve Gramsci on countless occasions: not, now, for his theory of 'civil society', but for his theory of the state. Here things become highly confused, for a very simple reason. Gramsci, who is a revolutionary, knows well that taking state power is the key question in every revolution; he has learnt this from Marx, Lenin and the whole Marxist tradition. The problem that presents itself to him is that of somehow attaching his theory of 'civil society' – and thus his own discovery (namely, that 'civil society' is not the infrastructure or simply 'needs' (Hegel), that is, the pure economy, but, rather, the whole set of 'hegemonic apparatuses') – to the essentials of the Marxist theory of the state.

Here again, neglecting both the infrastructure and the reproduction of the relations of production, he applies his basic method – description of the facts – and his philosophical master premise: every fact is historical, and therefore every political fact too bears its own light within itself. All one needs is an exact description and well-chosen comparisons. All one needs, in sum, is to see well, to read well. But what does Gramsci 'see'? He sees, thus inaugurating a veritable 'political theory' in the bourgeois sense, that all states comprise two 'moments': on the one hand, the moment of force or coercion or violence or dictatorship, on the other, the moment of hegemony, consensus, agreement. In the first 'moment', we will of course recognize what Marx and Lenin call the repressive state apparatus. But in the second?

Gramsci reveals that what is hiding behind it is 'civil society'! This is to be expected, because, made up as it is of hegemonic apparatuses, its function is hegemony: obtaining consensus. It is, however, unexpected, because Gramsci has explained to us that the second moment of the state is distinct from the state, since it is 'private'. One is therefore at a loss: How can something that was explicitly conceived of as *outside the state* constitute the second 'moment' of the state? Might the state have one of its 'moments', one of its decisive functions, 'outside itself'?

That an essential 'moment' *of the state*, the second, should assume a form of existence *external to the state* is something that strikes me as extremely interesting. But then one should perhaps try to *think* this paradoxical relationship, and assign it a relatively correct concept. I have for my part attempted to do so by proposing that we use the term ideological state apparatuses, a formula that has a twofold advantage. Firstly, it does away with the contradiction 'in the state/outside the state'. Secondly, it inscribes in the corresponding concept a formal indication of the hegemonic apparatuses' mode of functioning – *ideology*.[46] This has the further consequence of forcing us to begin to think the materiality of the ideologies.

Manifestly, however, Gramsci is not at all inclined to confront his own contradiction. On the contrary, he is inclined to leave it as is. This is not just because he contents himself with describing what he sees and does not go on to think it – at least, refuses to think it when he stumbles upon this contradiction – but also because *he needs this contradiction*. As we shall soon see, he needs it for political reasons.

Let us provisionally put this contradiction in brackets, then, and follow Gramsci in his reflections upon his descriptions. For to say that there are two moments in the state, that of force and that of hegemony, is extremely meagre. How can this idea be fleshed out? It might be imagined that Gramsci will, at the very least, embark on an analysis of each of these two 'moments', that he will help us discover something new in the state. But no; not one word more. Everything novel and important that there is to say has been said about 'civil society'. We shall get nothing else.

Or, rather, we shall get something else after all: something like imaginary variations (corresponding, every time, to empirical historical facts) for the purpose of seeing what relationships can possibly obtain between the state's two 'moments'. For it 'leaps to the eye' that, with different 'dosages' of force and hegemony (be it recalled that we still do not know how this hegemony is exercised), we shall find ourselves in the presence of different types of state. Let

me point out, right away, the two extremes on the scale of
variations. At one extreme, we have a state in which force
overwhelmingly predominates and hegemony is practically
non-existent: for example, Czarist Russia, where force
was overwhelming and 'civil society' was 'gelatinous'. At
the other extreme, force is reduced as far as possible and
hegemony is as great as possible; for example – but lo and
behold, the example is our old friend the well-balanced
ethical state, for which, or for its look-alikes, Gramsci
comes up with fine Aristotelian formulas of the type: 'a
proper balance'.

Gramsci is not finished with Marx and Lenin, however,
and with the difficulty of thinking their thought in his
own. For he is well aware that the state is also an
'instrument' (he does not care much for this word) in the
dominant class's hands, hence that, behind this description
of variable doses of force and hegemony, another, far more
serious, question is posed: that of the class domination
exercised by means of the state, a class domination which,
in Marxism, traditionally bears the name 'class dictatorship'. This means that the state comes second with
respect to this class domination or dictatorship. (It should
be clear that class dictatorship by no means designates
political forms, which are variable and can range from
political dictatorship to parliamentary democracy or mass
democracy, but the whole set of the dominant class's forms
of domination, which are at once economic, political and
ideological.) This inevitably confronts Gramsci with a very
serious problem: How is he to find, using the concepts
to which he wishes to confine himself – his own – the
wherewithal with which to think this primacy of class
domination in its entirety over the means par excellence of
achieving it, the state?

At this decisive point, Gramsci refuses to talk about
class dictatorship or even class domination. He is intent
on sticking exclusively to his own concepts, force and
hegemony. What does he proceed to do? He proceeds to
'inflate' the concept of hegemony out of all proportion,
so as to make it play, practically, the role of a substitute
for the concept of dominant class or class dictatorship.

This is, it must be said, a rhetorical and theoretical tour de force! For he had unambiguously located hegemony in the 'hegemonic apparatuses' that constitute civil society. Even if we did not know how hegemony was produced, we knew, at least, to which 'private', restricted domain it belonged. Now we see that it is not only associated with the state, even while remaining external to it, but that it will ultimately encompass *the whole state*. In order to be Marxist and Leninist, Gramsci ends up thinking *the state as hegemony*, or, rather, as the phenomenon of a hegemony that embraces and dominates it, although it is never a question, in all these 'analyses', of either class domination or class dictatorship.

But we have not finished with hegemony. For, as a Marxist and a Leninist, Gramsci, although he says little about this, knows, after all, that the class struggle exists and that its stakes are the state. However, since he has ended up thinking the state as hegemony (one clearly senses a class behind this hegemony that stands over and above the state alone), how can he represent the class struggle of which the state is the stakes? He finds the formula: he will talk not about a struggle for hegemony, but about a 'struggle of hegemonies', as if the class struggle were not also a struggle of forces against other forces and, above all, as if things were played out between 'hegemonies', as if 'the hegemony' of the dominated classes really could 'struggle' against the 'hegemony' of the dominant class.[47]

What 'leaps to the eye' in this whole line of argument, which is very consciously set out in Gramsci, is that, at the level of words, of concepts, and therefore of thought, we here witness a veritable operation of substitution of the sort at which Gramsci is so adept. We start out from the distinction force/hegemony and, by the end, force has disappeared. Doubtless the term 'hegemony' stands in for the concept of class domination or dictatorship *at this point*, yet we once again find ourselves before an empirical fact: that is just how it is, class domination is exercised in forms in which there clearly is force, but force is absorbed in hegemony, in other words, in the consensus obtained by the dominant class, just as the policeman is absorbed both in his function (regulating traffic) and in traffic (which he regulates). In sum, there is force in a well-regulated state, but it is a part of everyone and goes unnoticed.

It will be recalled that I envisaged this case – an invisible force that does not intervene – and that I said it intervened through its absence (or, if one likes, its near-total dissolution in the people), something that holds, concretely, for a number of ideological apparatuses; they run, in this way, on an invisible force, *the mere existence of which* makes possible its visible effects, which are quite pleasant (consider 'gentle psychiatry', education and the like).

However, if we ask what remains once we have reached the end point represented by the state, we come to see that it is no accident that Gramsci has said so little about ideology and nothing about the cause of the hegemonic effects of the 'hegemonic apparatuses'. Contrary to what might be supposed, this 'hegemony', which ultimately sums up the whole state, has nothing to do with ideology. This particular hegemony is not the peaceful, universal reign of values and ideas which are said to impose themselves on everyone and which everyone accepts. No. This hegemony is *political* through and through, in the Gramscian sense of the term, which Gramsci never defines. This politics is at once the 'lived experience' of all men, and also the fact that this 'lived experience' comprises their essence, the essence of their *activity*, which, it will be remembered, is the essence of every philosophy (and I remind you that everything is philosophy). This politics is, at the same time – this second determination is the cause of the first – 'politics in the command post', in the consciousness, to begin with, of those who engage in politics, that is, to various degrees, all men. The fact that it is still a matter of politics in the Gramscian sense, that is to say, in an empiricist sense, is crucial to understanding its destiny; yet this is truly the thought of a politician and a Marxist who knows very well that a beautiful ethical unity will not come about all by itself, that it has to be brought about at the end of a long process of struggle (political activity) in which the party's intervention is indispensable. It is the thought of a politician and a Marxist who knows very well that ideological values are not the motor of history and that they are only imposed on people in 'the well-regulated state' by 'politics'.

The question that then arises is: Why was it necessary to deduce this end result – which is so classic, tells us nothing that is not already in Marx and Lenin, and is, after all, quite meagre – why was it necessary to deduce it from a system of thought and concepts foreign to Marx and Lenin? Why was it necessary to proceed by way of all these 'discoveries' that efface themselves as we discover them one after the next and move on? Why was it necessary to proceed by way of all these mental acrobatics on hegemony in order to arrive at such simple, well-known results? The reason lies elsewhere.

It lies, once again, in hegemony (the third sense of the word)! For Gramsci is the first Marxist theorist to have insisted so heavily on the necessity, for the dominated class, of securing 'its hegemony' before taking power. All the classics of Marxism had said, clearly and well, two things: 1) the vanguard of the working class must extend its influence as far as possible and win the greatest possible number of adherents over to 'its ideas', not just in the working class, but also among the petty bourgeoisie and intellectuals; 2) the party of the working class must extend its influence, its 'hegemony', over the neighbouring mass organizations and conclude alliances with them, which are essential to taking power. If it fails to do so, the proletariat's 'solo' runs the risk of becoming a 'swan song'.[48] Gramsci subscribes to these two theses, but he adds a third: the working class must become hegemonic throughout society 'before taking power'.

What, then, might 'hegemony' mean? The answer that Gramsci gives, as a good Marxist politician, is clear. It is not only a matter of extending the influence of the party's ideas, and their audience, to the whole of society, which would then become, miraculously, Marxist before being socialist. Nor is it a matter of seizing control of the state, since we are merely laying the groundwork for conquering it. It is a matter of seizing control of power centres in civil society, of seizing control of civil society itself.

This can only be understood from the way civil society is positioned vis-à-vis the state. For we can, according to Gramsci, picture the arrangement [*dispositif*] of the state's two 'moments' with the help of a spatial metaphor. The state is at the centre, like a keep or a fortress; force resides in the walls and behind them. Encircling this fortress-state and reaching a long way into the countryside is an extensive network of trenches and bunkers: this network is civil society. We can readily understand that this network is 'gelatinous' when the state is nothing but force. In that case, a frontal assault is the only way to capture it: the Winter Palace. We 'see', however, that the network is dense and deeply rooted in our states. Well then: one has to gain control of it step by step, one trench at a time, and to capture the whole of civil society. The state will then be defenceless and one will be able to make one's way into it.[49]

We see the bedrock of Gramsci's thought here. It is a *strategy*, an alternative strategy as our Italian friends like to put it, for taking power in 'developed' capitalist countries possessing a powerful network of bunkers, that is, a powerful civil society. This is the 'war of position'.[50] This strategy of the 'war of position' of Gramscian inspiration today inspires all the communist parties professing 'Eurocommunism', of which Paul Laurent has publicly taken the defence in his article in the [13 May 1978] *L'Humanité*.[51] One understands why this strategy merits interest and 'reflection'.[52]

I should like, for my part, to make the following remarks.

When Gramsci talks about 'civil society', he in fact defines it in two different ways. I have not referred to the second, in order to give every chance to the problematic coherency of his thought. Gramsci, however, does not limit the definition of civil society to the ensemble of 'hegemonic apparatuses'; for, if we strip away the state, if we strip away the hegemonic apparatuses, is nothing left? What is left is, precisely, the infrastructure, about which Gramsci is so reserved; or, if one prefers, what is left is the economic, or commercial enterprises of all sorts, and consumption and family life. Do these 'organizations' too form part of civil society? Gramsci does not say. We could say so at a pinch, declaring enterprises, families and so on to be 'hegemonic apparatuses'. Gramsci realizes, confusedly, that that would not work very well: it's fine as far as families are concerned (I have said so, for my part),[53] but, in the enterprises, a little something goes on which, even if there is indeed hegemony in them, must also be taken into account: *the extraction of surplus value*. Gramsci knows enough about the infrastructure not to talk about it and, as well, to avoid putting it in civil society. Thus there is an enormous blank in Gramsci's system: everything bearing on the relation of production, exploitation, and everything constituting their material condition: capital, imperialism (about which Gramsci says not a word), labour-power, its reproduction and so on. When Gramsci evokes 'civil society' in the broad, hence classic, hence bourgeois, sense (everything that is not the state), he contents himself with pronouncing the word: the reason is that he needs it in passing, to meet the needs of a line of reasoning – yet *he never goes* into the reality, details, mechanism and role ('determinant in the last instance')[54] of this huge blank.

3

Gramsci or Machiavelli?

It is here that Gramsci's truly unconditional admiration for Machiavelli acquires all its meaning.[1] For what did Machiavelli do? He was the very first person to talk about the class struggle and the active burghers' [*bourgeois*] class domination of the idle, usurious nobility. He showed that the *productive* bourgeoisie's class domination could be ensured by just one determinate political form, the absolute monarchy of 'one individual'[2] who relies for support on the bourgeoisie, not the nobility, in order to found a national state and govern the people through virtue and ruse, as well as through the capacity to subordinate (moral) virtue to ruse and feint (and even the worst methods of treachery and cruelty).[3] This capacity bears the unique, untranslatable name *virtù* in Machiavelli. Everything is already there in him: the theory of the state and its two moments, 'beast' (force) and man (consensus).[4] Yet there is far more in him than in Gramsci, because, in Machiavelli, the beast *divides into two*, since it is, at one and the same time, lion (brute force) and fox (ruse and feint),[5] and since the fox is, ultimately, *virtù* alone, or the capacity to make use of force and consensus (hegemony) at will, in accordance with the imperatives of the conjuncture (the 'opportunity', which may or may not be 'good fortune').[6] There is, however, still more than this in Machiavelli, since the capacity for ruse ultimately comes down to the ability to feign, to the power to pretend (to seem virtuous when one is not and, above all, and this is much harder, to seem virtuous when one is).[7]

With that, Machiavelli goes much further than Gramsci. He shows that ideology (above all, the ideological representation of the 'figure of the Prince', in which it is unified as the ideology of the state 'represented' by the Prince as we see him, crowned with the aureole of his prestige and, literally, of his 'image', which is obviously in excess of anything that can be observed of his features, bearing or gestures, there only to serve that 'image')[8] is constitutive of all state power, be it in the form of religion, needed to create the best possible consensus, in any case the consensus best suited to maintaining a unified army,[9] but also a people, since it produces the best and surest, because *the most constant*, of the forms of consensus among the masses of the people. This takes the form of the *military amalgamation* which, mobilizing all the men of the people in the army, and prioritizing the infantry (common men, first and foremost peasants) over the cavalry (the traditional corps of the nobles, who own horses), is not just a military principle, but also a means of producing ideological transformation effects in the citizen-soldiers; it is a veritable school of politics that teaches them, in actual practice, the unity of voluntarily accepted discipline, while also teaching them to treat the nobles on their horses as they deserve to be treated: as the auxiliaries, not the leaders, of the true soldiers, the productive citizens.[10]

One readily sees how impoverished Gramsci, who exalted Machiavelli, is in comparison with his teacher. For Gramsci never affirmed, unlike Machiavelli, the primacy of the 'moment' of force (the army) over 'hegemony' in the state. Overtly present in Machiavelli, force appears in Gramsci only in order to pave the way for its pure and simple disappearance in the concept of the state as hegemony. Moreover, when he did invoke force, Gramsci never considered it to be anything other than brute, naked force (the Machiavellian figure of the 'lion' that is purely and simply brawn and has nothing between the ears). Gramsci never suspected that force might be productive, fecund and well-suited to taking its place in a strategy in which it can produce hegemony effects (political education of the citizenry through amalgamation in the army). Gramsci never suspected that the beast might be something other than force (the lion): namely, ruse, the fox, that singular animal infinitely more intelligent than 'man' (who represents recognition of moral virtues and the good), because its reason consists entirely in the ability to *feign*. And Gramsci never understood that feint is consubstantial with the state, or, rather, with the Prince's political strategy, and that its effect is above all to produce, for the people's consumption, the representation or 'image' of the Prince without which there is no state power; for, to exist, this power must be recognized by the people, which can recognize state power only by recognizing itself in it – precisely by recognizing itself in the ideological 'image' of the Prince as the head of a state rendered incontestable by that image.

With that, Machiavelli responds to Gramsci's silence on the question as to what might make the 'hegemonic apparatuses' run. He responds to Gramsci's complete silence on *ideology*, considered with regard to its major function, its political function. With that, Machiavelli does not just broach the theory of ideology and recognition of the organic necessity of a state ideology if the state is to exercise its hegemony, hence recognition of the fact that hegemony runs on [*fonctionne sur*] ideology and that it is not enough to define hegemony by its hegemony effects (that is a tautology), since it must, rather, be defined by its 'motor', *the ideology that is organically bound up with the state*.

With that, Machiavelli puts us on the track of a concept like the concept of the 'Ideological State Apparatus', as the concept indispensable to understanding one whole aspect of the functioning of the state as well as the political, and therefore material, status of ideology. And, when it is a question of ideology, Machiavelli – who, obviously, does not employ the term – does not content himself with the word (or its equivalents) or with *describing* the thing that the word designates, as Gramsci always does; rather, he actually embarks on the concrete research that leads to a possible theory of the ideologies.

He embarks on it not just by way of his theory of the conditions and forms of the feint that produces the ideology of the 'image' of the Prince, but also, and above all, by way of his theory of force as well-suited to producing ideological effects which, far from being violent effects, are not just consensus effects, but also effects of the transformation of ideology in all the citizens of the people assembled in the army in which the nobles astride their horses are demoted to the second rank.

As Foucault says so well, force can be productive. He might have an interest in rereading Machiavelli on this point, so as to progress in his research without losing his way in a generalization in which all lions are grey. In any case, the idea that force can be productive of ideology is of direct concern to any theory of the ideologies, for it is a very good way of saying what we are trying to say again more than five hundred [*sic*] years later and one hundred years after Marx: that one can never hope to establish a theory of the ideologies without considering the fact that ideology is not 'ideas', but a certain materiality, that of the 'apparatuses' which realize it; and, as soon as we start talking about both materiality and apparatuses, it becomes only too clear that, like Machiavelli, we are talking about force.

To be sure, this force is not the lion's, but the fox's, and the fox's force consists in knowing how to make wise use of the lion's in order to produce either effects of physical violence or effects of feint (or representation, as Claude Lefort rightly says; of ideology, I would say; but there is no reason to quibble over words here: we agree).[11] The fact that Machiavelli thinks the twofold capacity of state power as 'beast' through the figure of the lion on the one hand, and that of the fox on the other, is of the highest theoretical importance. The fact that he thus situates these political capacities wholly outside the subjectivity of the individual-Prince in order to think them as the

non-psychological concepts of the lion and fox – the fact
that he abstracts completely, after all, from the individual-
Prince who, he earnestly hopes, will found an Italian
nation-state, and the fact that this abstraction is among the
political conditions for the Prince's advent (this *must* be,
not *can* be, someone unknown, suddenly surging up from
some unpredictable corner of Italy, with no rightful claim
to political authority to vindicate – meaning that there is
absolutely nothing to be expected, as far as founding the
nation-state is concerned, from any of the existing Princes
or regimes, or, in particular, from any of the existing
republics, since they all belong to the old feudal world that
has to be toppled, whose *state forms* have to *be destroyed*
to found a new state under a new prince): all this proves
that Machiavelli thinks as a politician and as a materialist,
and that he knows, as someone who thinks under the
domination of 'humanism', but in radical opposition to it,
that politics is a matter not of individuals, but of strategy,
line, and the right means for realizing this strategy.

Notwithstanding all the appearances that impose, on
superficial readers who have a stake in such readings,
the constant presence of the individual who embodies
the Prince, with his virtues and vices, Machiavelli knows
and says that if the form of state power has to take the
form of an individual, it is because political conditions
require this state form as the only possible solution to the
problem of the destruction of the feudal states. Indeed,
this individual-Prince is so little 'a man' that Machiavelli
speaks of the 'strange adventure',[12] for an individual, of
becoming Prince, that is, of ceasing to be a man in order
to become an unheard-of creature, a man-lion-fox, a triad
or topography with no centre, no 'ego', to unify these three
'moments' or 'instances'. This creature is, in other words,
never a 'man', that is, a moral subject, unless it *seems* to
be one. (If, in addition, it happens to be one, so much the
better; but this is a great danger, for the great difficulty
stems from the fact that the same 'man' must absolutely be
able to cease to be a 'man' whenever the situation requires
– must 'learn to be able to be not good' when it is necessary
to be harsh, trampling all the moral virtues underfoot.[13])

No, the Prince is not an individual, a human *subject* capable of virtue or vice by nature or reason. The Prince is a system of instances lacking a central subject, lacking the subjective unity that would realize the synthesis of his objective functions in him. And since the Prince is nothing without the strategic utilization of this system of instances, without their strategic mobilization, we might just as well say that the Prince is a political strategy and, as such, a 'process without a subject',[14] for he does no more than represent, in the strategy that he is, the strategy of the productive bourgeoisie's struggle against the feudal states that must be destroyed and replaced by a new state.

To say so is once again to speak of ideology, to continue to speak of ideology. For this strategy cannot be effected unless the productive people recognizes itself in it, recognizes it as *its own*. Machiavelli has nothing of a utopian about him.[15] He does not think up *a strategy for the people* while 'holding monologues' 'seated at his desk' (Georges Marchais), that is, in the privacy of his peaceful abode.[16] At the limit, Machiavelli would say – and certain accents in his texts as well as the conditions of their composition and non-publication confirm this impression – that it is not even he who thinks, the individual-subject Machiavelli. He himself says that the whole of political history thinks in him, and we need but look to see that it is true: it is Rome that thinks aloud in his work, and the Kingdom of France, and the Italian political 'misère', its void and its nothingness that speak here, and the pathetic appeal which, on all sides, rises up from the Italian popular masses, the appeal to have done with these feudal states and to build what France and Spain have succeeded in building: a national state.

It is not enough to say, however, that it is not Machiavelli who thinks in his crucial problem, but, rather, Italian history and the Italian people. The strategy presented (and we can say: Machiavelli *is* this strategy as much as the Prince is) must be received by the popular masses, and they must recognize themselves in it.[17] This strategy itself must therefore be presented in the form of an *ideology* producing these effects of consensus and conviction in order to rally the masses to the idea of rallying around a Prince about whom absolutely nothing is known, except that he will have to realize this strategy to be this Prince.

Ideology is, therefore, vital not just to the existence and functioning of the state, but also to the presentation of this strategy to the people – to its popular representation. A kind of hegemony has to come about before the new state is constituted: the hegemony of the idea of this strategy. It must win the masses over before the advent of the new state; otherwise, the new state cannot be constituted. Even if a *virtuoso* individual applies himself to the task, and even if he has all the good fortune in the world at his beck and call, as long as the people fails to recognize him as the one capable of realizing this strategy – in other words, as long as the people is not imbued with the idea of this strategy in order to judge the Prince – the cause will be a lost cause.

How can one anticipate ideological effects that can be created only by the new state, when it is necessary to produce them before the new state is created simply so that it can be? This is a circle that Gramsci resolved with his thesis about realizing hegemony before the capture of state power. The question of the validity of his thesis aside, Gramsci had appearances, at least, going for him – the appearances of the absence of the circle, since he disposed of the means of constituting this hegemony prior to the constitution of a new state: the communist party. Gramsci says that the party is the 'modern Prince'. He is wrong.

To begin with, the party is not a Prince. By that, I do not mean that it is not an individual. I mean that it is an altogether different strategy: not the bourgeois strategy of the destruction of the feudal states and the foundation of a new, exploitative national state, but the strategy of the destruction of the bourgeois state and the foundation of a revolutionary state that is to do away with exploitation and oppression. Secondly, Gramsci plays on words; he supposes – finding support for his supposition in a whole series of expressions of Machiavelli's that he takes literally, when they should be taken with the greatest possible caution by anyone who knows what a Fox they come from

– that the sudden emergence of the Prince will produce the ideology that will have made his advent possible. In short, he does away with every trace, in Machiavelli, of the issue that he has himself raised: that hegemony (or a certain type of hegemony) must be realized beforehand for the Prince to be possible.

In fact, as a conscious politician, Machiavelli well and truly accepts this contradiction. And he resolves it with the *sole* means at his disposal, like the politician he is, who counts only on the real. His solution is to have a strategy of the Prince's strategy and, as such, to behave like a *man-lion-fox*.

A *man*: he is a man by virtue of his intellectual honesty, which we discern in all his arguments, in their rigour and in his vast, unchallengeable documentation, for we never catch him making a mistake. A *man*: he is a man by virtue of his passion for the common good, for Italy's salvation. A *man*: he is a man by virtue of his touching compassion for all the misfortunes afflicting the people of his country: invasions, perpetual wars, foreign domination, exactions, crimes, exploitation of the productive burghers by the nobles and of the *Ciompi*[18] by the wealthy burghers. A *man*: he is a man by virtue of his passion, contained or unleashed, the extraordinary passion that inspires, at the end of *The Prince* and in a dozen other passages in his work, *the appeal* to rally to the cause that he addresses to all the men of his country, so that, recognizing the strategy that can save them, they unite at last.[19]

A *lion*: he is a lion in that he puts his force in the service of his combat. A weak force, to tell the truth, nearly nothing: practical experience of politics, responsibilities in public affairs, albeit subaltern ones, even if he has had dealings with most of the great men of his day, a few relationships with powerful people that have, however, disappeared (either the relationships or the people) and also with a man who was truly someone after his own heart, Cesare Borgia, but who missed his chance for the simple reason that he was delirious with fever in the swamps of Ravenna when he would have had to be in Rome,[20] and a few friendships with high-born young men bursting with talent whom he entertained towards the end under the trees of a garden. In sum, nothing or nearly nothing.

A *fox*: it is a very different story here! Together with the 'man', this constitutes Machiavelli's true force, his greatest force. A *fox*: as the man-Prince must 'be capable of being not good', *the fox, who is, in his essence, feint, must be capable of not feigning*, and that is Machiavelli's whole force, his trump card, which he never stops playing. In a world ruled by ruse and feint, in which it is clear, in view of the crudity of the procedure or its results, that everyone feigns, that 'public opinion', hence feigning, rules the world,[21] that feigning reigns supreme as a method of governing and oppressing men, *Machiavelli's feint will consist in not feigning*.

And this is clearly a feint, since everyone who entertains this suspicion will say that Machiavelli merely 'feigned' to tell the truth, in order to say, in reality, something completely different: that he 'feigned' to address himself to the Prince in order to talk to him about 'tyranny', when his real intention was to address himself to men and talk to them about 'freedom'. This is what the majority of authors in the eighteenth century and the Risorgimento said. For them, Machiavelli 'feigned' to teach principles of government to princes only in order to enlighten the people about their practices. Machiavelli 'feigned' to be a monarchist (in *The Prince*), but only in order to plead in favour of the republic (in the *Discourses*).

There is, however, no feint at all in Machiavelli, and that, precisely, is his feint. There is so little feint that he examines *every case* (*The Prince*). So as not to omit a single one, he does not proceed, as Descartes will later do, by 'enumerations so complete' that it is certain that nothing has been forgotten (for one must be sure that *all the cases* have been assembled).[22] He uses a different method, which I have proposed to call 'thinking at the extremes'.[23] Thus Machiavelli reasons by examining *the possible limit-cases*, by supposing that they are real and studying them.

Thus we have the limit-case that has it that, in order to govern them, 'one must suppose all men to be wicked',[24] an affirmation of which Machiavelli offers not a single concrete example (this is never the case for him elsewhere); yet it is by thinking in terms of this limit-hypothesis that one makes sure to think the worst possible case, and if one solves that limit-problem, then all the other problems will be lesser problems, and easy to solve. Thus we have the limit case of the individual-Prince: Machiavelli thinks in terms of the limit-case of an anonymous, utterly unknown individual, without force or power, hence without a state, a man descended of no one knows whom, suddenly surging up from no one knows where no one knows when. All one asks of him is that he have *virtù*, that is, a kind of powerful political instinct that makes him throw himself on the occasion that presents itself in order to 'seize' it; and, if this occasion is 'fortunate',[25] in other words, propitious, an instinct that will inspire him to do whatever he must to seize it ('take fortune as you would take a woman').[26] Then if *virtù* and good fortune persist, or, at least, if *virtù* endures in the man when good fortune leaves him in the lurch, a possible future will be open before him until such time as he lays the foundations of a state that 'lasts',[27] endowing it with laws that ensure its duration.

I do not think we need search any further for the fox in Machiavelli. *He discovered an absolutely unprecedented feint in the ideological domain*, that is, a form of discourse that produces unprecedented ideological effects: *it consists in not feigning in anything*. To be sure, he has occasion to disguise his thoughts as a precaution, but to disguise is not to feign: Machiavelli never feigns. *The ideological presentation* of known reality presents itself in him in the paradoxical form of *a simple presentation of known reality*. He contents himself with 'saying what happens in fact',[28] not in the sense of the law, which states fact a priori, that is, which defines legal fact, but in the *political* sense of the class struggle as conditioned by a state power organically bound up with a state ideology.[29]

In this world, in which everything is regulated by state power and the state ideology (the Prince's official image + religion + the effects of amalgamation in the army), in this world in which everyone 'feigns', not at all out of

malice or vice, but because *it is the law* that state power
and the state ideology impose on everyone, Machiavelli
consciously chooses to occupy a completely unexpected
place. He 'chooses' not to feign. *He chooses to reject
the law that dominates everyone*, the Prince included –
indeed, the Prince first and foremost. This means that he
is unwilling to position himself not only on the adversary's
terrain, but even on that of existing society; or, rather, it
means that he is not only unwilling to position himself
on existing society's terrain because existing society is
his adversary. He 'shifts ground' (to borrow a term from
Themistocles that will later, at the unconscious level, speak
powerfully to Marx),[30] deliberately positioning himself
elsewhere, on another terrain.

Just as one must be on the plain to contemplate the
majesty of the mountains, so 'one must be people to
know Princes'. On another terrain: on the plain. With
the people, or, rather, by becoming-people. This 'other
terrain' is the one, and the only one, from which one
can 'know Princes'.[31] The people's terrain is thus also the
terrain of knowledge. And it is *from true knowledge* that
Machiavelli expects *the ideological effect*, the only one
in his power, which is necessary to prepare the popular
masses for the strategy of the New Prince.

The truth [*la vérité*] *told* will be disconcerting; it
will shake minds out of their lethargy, leaving them in
perplexity and contradiction. But *contradiction* is already
there, in the class struggle. Machiavelli does not invent
it; he relies on it, orienting and inflecting it in ways
favourable to the bourgeois class struggle. If he tells the
truth [*le vrai*], it is because it already exists. Once told,
the truth will carve its path through the contradiction that
it reinforces by intervening in it. And if a man endowed
with *virtù* turns up [*se rencontre*], one who knows how to
embark on this strategy because he has understood it or
who simply embarks on it by instinct, and if he is favoured
by great good fortune, then – who knows? – something
like the New State may begin to emerge. ...

Once again, as a true politician, Machiavelli refuses
to behave like a 'prophet unarmed', like Savonarola,

preaching utopias to the exalted masses.[32] He does not want to be a prophet; he execrates anything resembling God, his church, his priests, and his visionaries, since a religious or an idealist conception of politics always culminates in tyrannicide and/or massacre. He entertains no illusions about the arms at his disposal: he is all but unarmed, except that one arm is left him, just one: knowing how to refuse to feign at all times and, simply, tell the truth. He does not believe that the truth, once told, will by itself take possession of the world, driving the shadows of error back before the bright light of truth, as the ideologues of the Enlightenment thought. He knows that telling the truth is all he can do, and he knows very well that that will not go very far, because a great many other conditions are required for truth to penetrate the masses: political conditions, which it is not in an isolated intellectual's power to think that he can ever bring about. Machiavelli is a materialist: even while choosing to tell the truth without ever feigning, he never succumbs to the madness of the omnipotence of ideas.

Yet if Machiavelli is, as we just saw, far in advance of Gramsci on several points, on another, he and Gramsci have exactly the same position. Machiavelli, if he discusses politics extremely well, discusses nothing *but* politics. If he refers to those who work and those who are idle (the nobles), and if he refers to those whose condition is more wretched than that of those who work (by the working population, he means the productive bourgeoisie and petty bourgeoisie: manufacturers, traders, shopkeepers, productive landowners, farmers and so on),[33] the *Ciompi*, wool-workers who, even at this early date, were wage-workers in one of Italy's islands of capitalist production,[34] Machiavelli never alludes to what is vulgarly known as[35]

_____ criticism. And _____

criticize _____ for this lacuna, lest we lapse into the absurdity of trying him on retroactive charges) is not without impact on his conception of the class struggle, the conflict which, in Machiavelli, opposes two 'humours', those of the 'fat' and the 'lean'.[36] *The idea of exploitation is excluded from this conception.* Machiavelli explains class struggle with reference to, not exploitation, but *proprietorship*, hence the *desire* of the haves to have still more and of the have-nots to have. Since he limits himself to the juridical notion of proprietorship, without going beyond its bounds, it is the *relationship* of proprietorship to non-proprietorship which becomes the explanation for proprietorship and non-proprietorship. This relationship is a relationship of 'desire'.[37]

Thus desire is at the root of class struggle: the desire to possess more and the desire to dominate more, on the one hand, and, on the other, the desire to possess something and not be dominated.[38] This goes hand in hand with the arresting view that *the desire of the haves and the great is the 'cause' of the division of desire, hence of class struggle,*[39] and that, in the class struggle, it is *the class struggle of the dominant class that is the motor of the class struggle as a whole, the class struggle of the dominated included* – a truth that would not be rediscovered until Marx. The fact is, however, that nothing is said about what happens beneath the surface of proprietorship, hence beneath the surface of 'desire'. The fact is that everything is presented in the mode of the 'that's how it is', the empiricist mode dear to Gramsci. And the fact is that everything that happens in a 'society' comes down purely and simply to politics, as in Gramsci.

This analysis was, I believe, needed to make it possible to understand the underlying reasons for which Gramsci spontaneously recognizes himself in Machiavelli. (In Gramsci's view, Machiavelli is clearly his only precursor in his mode of thought – Machiavelli, not Marx.)[40] _____

_____

_____   _____

_____ that he is a politician, not just because he acknowledges the 'autonomy of the political'[41] vis-à-vis morality and religion, not just because he opens up the possibility of a 'science of politics', that bourgeois 'discipline' that has precious little that is Marxist about it and is dear to Gramsci, but also *because, like Gramsci, he reduces* everything to politics;

because, for him, everything is political, which means, put plainly, that there is nothing beyond politics worthy of serious attention, *above all* when one wants to engage in politics.

By upholding this thesis practically (not theoretically) in his writings, Machiavelli provides Gramsci with the opportunity to find himself a father, his *one and only* father,[42] while, anachronistically, skipping over Marx. For we cannot reproach Machiavelli for erecting his entire œuvre on the basis of an immense blank (that of the infrastructure, the relation of production, of reproduction, and so on). However, the fact that the entire œuvre produced by Gramsci, who thinks three hundred years after Machiavelli,[43] but also seventy years after a certain Marx, *also has, at its basis, the same immense blank*, is, after all, a rather strange affair, above all when one bears in mind that Gramsci claims to be a follower of Marx as well (albeit on different grounds, not on the grounds of the 'theory of the political'). It is all too clear that the immense blank in Gramsci, who thinks after Marx and Lenin and claims to be a follower of theirs, can in no sense have the same significance as the same blank in Machiavelli's œuvre, three hundred years earlier. *That which Machiavelli could not have seen and understood was in fact quite simply obliterated and deleted by Gramsci.* And as nothing happens by accident, especially not at this level, we may say that it was *deliberately* obliterated and deleted. To what ends? That is another story.

Once he has left out [enough to produce] this immense blank and forgotten the fact that it determines, in the last instance, everything he discusses – 'his' civil society, 'his' hegemonic apparatuses, 'his' two-moment state (in the sense in which one says a 'two-stroke' engine), 'his' class dictatorship, as well as politics and every class struggle strategy, Gramsci can tell us whatever he likes, can describe and compare historical examples in the 'You want examples? Here you go' mode ('one would have to produce a complete enumeration ...'), can draw the 'moral' of history or give history moral lessons [*tirer la 'morale' de l'histoire ou la lui faire*], can combine his little equations on the state in order to prepare his[44] _____ _____

---

these are so many combinations and speculations *in the void*. Every society has a base; otherwise, it is in the void. Every demonstration must master, by means of thought, the 'base' of that which it discusses; otherwise, it is in the void.

What Marxist would fail to understand, even if he finds Gramsci's exceptional intelligence, his sense of detail and nuance and, naturally, his anti-dogmatism and anti-Stalinism appealing and convincing, that *it is absolutely impossible to accept the 'conclusions' of someone who leaves out what is 'determinant in the last instance' for Marxism, as Gramsci does in all his reasoning: namely, exploitation, its conditions, reproduction, and their incalculable consequences*? Above all when it is borne in mind that this 'Marxist' theorist fashions a conceptual edifice which, albeit quite original, is nevertheless ambiguous or contradictory throughout, only to discover all over again, at the end of the day, *two or three elementary truths* of Marxism, different only by virtue of a purely 'personal' formulation? Above all when it is borne in mind that he abandons 'what is determinant in the last instance' and fabricates the whole of his personal system in order to hold out an 'alternative' strategy to the workers' movement? *Can we take seriously, even for a moment, a strategy for the workers' movement that so blithely abstracts from what is 'determinant in the last instance'?* That is amateurism. It can be adventurism.

I understand that one can take very great pleasure in reading Gramsci, the same pleasure that he afforded himself in the horror of his prison: the pleasure of 'seeing' things directly, of multiplying historical examples of them for the pleasure of it, precisely the pleasure of which Gramsci was, in his misfortune, *deprived*.[45] _____
by their presence _____ the pleasure of being able to _____ everything *immediately*: to consume the object, that is to say, history, that is to say, politics, *like a delicacy*. A delicacy can be seen, it is there on the table; we see that it is delicious; and all we need do is reach

out, take it and taste it. Diderot said of Berkeley that he was 'a bishop to whom they brought his dinner ready to eat', for Berkeley never went into the kitchen and got his hands dirty cooking. There is something of this in Gramsci: things are ready, you need only see them to take and understand them. No need to go to the kitchen, to the scene of exploitation, where the dishes are prepared. As someone said, or could have: one can make anything and everything of a delicacy, even a strategy for amateurs – but not a strategy for the workers' movement.

If you doubt it, let me tell you: for, ultimately, from the standpoint of the masses, who have, to no avail, put their hearts and minds into it, that is the only thing that discriminates between all the theories. Look into the 'criterion of practice' and I'm pretty sure what you'll tell me. And all this is just getting off the ground in the world of the 'Eurocommunist' parties. Paul Laurent's benediction will surely give them a new burst of hope that they can get the better of all their little 'difficulties' thanks to the results of the conquest of 'civil society'.

4

Gramsci, Eurocommunism, Class Dictatorship

Since I have come out with the word, what relationship can we establish between Gramsci's thought and what is known as 'Eurocommunism'? We have just seen, in broad outline, what can be said about Gramsci's thought. What can be said about 'Eurocommunism'?

'Eurocommunism', if we put its geographical connotation to one side, can be very readily defined as a strategy for a democratic transition to a democratic socialism, or, still more exactly, as a strategy for the democratic preparation of an advanced democracy that will democratically pave the way for a democratic socialism. The essential feature of this strategy consists in the affirmation that the goal (democratic socialism) and the 'democratic' means are identical. In short, it consists in thinking strategy, tactics and means within the concept of democracy.[1]

I note in passing that the opposition of the end and the means, or even the contradiction between the end and the means, is universally considered to be a manifestation of intolerable cynicism and 'Machiavellianism'. (Yet Machiavelli *never* presents this opposition as such; he never thinks *in setting out from it*; he always thinks it and resolves it under determinate conditions that justify both its existence and its resolution.[2])

I likewise note that we have to do, in the identity of the end and the means, as well as in the strategy of Eurocommunism, in which democracy is at once end and means, with the same logic as in the contradiction between the end and the means, as long as we have not done what it is Machiavelli's merit to have done: as long as we have not truly thought the historical conditions that reveal the possibility of this unity, the variations in this relationship, and the differences covered by a single, undefined word, democracy.

All this in order to say that chances are good that the identity, proclaimed by the strategy of Eurocommunism, between the end and the means, which gives great satisfaction to all moralists and other idealists, is no more than an empty, that is to say, an adventurist proclamation, *as long as it has not been proven*, by means of a 'concrete analysis of the concrete situation' of the class struggle not only in the countries concerned, but in the whole world, capitalist imperialism and the 'socialist' countries included, that this strategy is something other than a figment of the imagination: that it is really possible, because its material, social, political and ideological conditions have been realized in the world.

The paradox of the current situation is *that no 'concrete analysis of the concrete situation' has been provided* to prove that the conditions for the strategy of Eurocommunism have been met. In saying this, I do not mean to say that these conditions do not exist, and thus that Eurocommunism is purely and simply democratic adventurism.[3] My claim is that we have no idea whether it is or not; that it could be, as long as it has not been proven that the historical conditions for this strategy have been realized; and that it would be, if concrete analysis proved that the supposed conditions for its realization were imaginary.

If support for Eurocommunism is not based on the positive conclusions of a concrete analysis, what *is* it based on? On two historical phenomena, in my opinion: the crisis of the international communist movement, and the movement of the popular masses. They intersect in their effect, the demand for democracy.

Clearly, the popular masses feel deeply that Eurocommunism is a disavowal of the non-democratic forms (they have been dictatorial and bloody; they continue to be oppressive) that hold sway in the countries of the East – that it takes a very clear political distance from the countries of the East[4] with respect to both the (non-democratic) means and also the end (a non-democratic 'socialism') whose spectacle these countries offer.[5] It took many long years for this disavowal to take form in the Western Communist Parties. Initially, in Italy, it was very cautiously cloaked in the appeal to Gramsci's thought, to his anti-dogmatism. It only just began to take form after the Twentieth Congress, but in extremely timid fashion even in Italy, and still more timidly elsewhere. It was not really openly affirmed, in still cautious forms, until after the invasion of Czechoslovakia (the military intervention in Hungary left the Communist Parties unmoved; in France, the upshot was the exclusion and departure of many militants, including some in leadership positions). Only in the past three years, with the exacerbation of the crisis of the international communist movement, has this disavowal taken the positive form of a condemnation of anti-democratic practices in the USSR and the other countries of the East, and the declaration of Eurocommunism, with a single word, at once a line and a universal slogan: democracy.

This whole development has taken place, very obviously, under pressure from the popular mass movement in the Western countries. In this regard, May 1968, contemporaneous with the Prague events, played a decisive part in shaping the PCF's attitude; in its Manifesto to the French about what 'the Communists want for France', the Party's Twenty-Second Congress truly took note of the demand for democracy emanating from the masses.[6] It incorporated this demand into its own strategy for accession to governmental power of the Union of the Left, sealed by the Common Programme, and it developed the now familiar themes of a democratic transition to a democratic socialism that was declared to be 'in France's national colours' so that no one would get things wrong: this socialism would not be 'in Moscow's colours'.

The French Party thus rallied to the strategy that the Italian Party had long since elaborated by way of a lengthy reflection on Gramsci's strategic thought. The strategic agreement on Eurocommunism, albeit still discreet, was sealed by an exchange of visits between Georges Marchais and Berlinguer.[7] It was heard by the Communist Party of Spain immediately it emerged from underground, and we even saw how the Spanish Party, which was the least powerful and had the least experience of this strategy, resolutely took the lead. It openly and unreservedly declared itself to be 'Eurocommunist',[8] something that neither the PCI nor the PCF had done, and it ultimately imposed this term on the other Communist Parties which, in Europe (England, etc.) and the rest of the world (Japan, Mexico, etc.), had embarked on a similar or the very same strategy, although they did not always call it by its name.

The strategy of Eurocommunism, however, has relied for support not just on the crisis of the international communist movement and the popular masses' 'democratic' demand, but on existing *theories* as well. This is truly paradoxical, for not only does there not exist a concrete analysis of the concrete situation proving that the strategy of Eurocommunism is possible; a *theory* of Eurocommunism does not exist, either (and for good reason: without a concrete analysis, a theory is impossible). Eurocommunism nevertheless finds support *in theories*, around which, for the moment, we shall not put inverted commas, although we shall see later, after examining the matter, whether we should put them around these theories. In which theories? In two theories.

To begin with, it finds support in Gramsci's thought. We will not be surprised, after what has been said about it, that Gramsci's thought should lend itself to justifying this strategy. For Gramsci authorizes Eurocommunism to think the capture of state power not as the result of a frontal assault, hence of popular violence that infringes all law and forgoes democracy, but as the result of a 'war of position' that aims to seize control of the civil society behind whose 'trenches and bunkers' the state is ensconced. Contrary to the frontal assault, which presupposes violence and, therefore, the violence done to (democratic) law, the conquest of 'civil society' will be effected 'step by step', 'by setting one stone on another' (Georges Marchais, opening speech at the Central Committee meeting),[9] by taking one position after another. Nothing requires that this gradual 'advance' come about by violent means. Everything makes it possible and necessary that it come about without violence, in keeping with existing law, hence in keeping with bourgeois democracy.

What does this conquest lead to, it will be asked? Who can prove that it is enough to invest the trenches which protect, in the plain, the fortress of the state for the state to let itself be captured in its turn, and by the same means?

This is the crucial question that Gramsci's theory of hegemony answers: not the theory of 'civil society' as the 'moment of hegemony' of a state whose other 'moment' is force, but the theory of the state as hegemony, or, rather, the theory that replaces the very notion of the state with the notion of hegemony. In this 'theory', which comprises one moment of the desperate reflection in which Gramsci searches for a theoretical solution to the political problems he has set himself, he ends up encompassing both class dictatorship and the whole state in the notion of hegemony, hence the two moments of the state (force and hegemony in the first sense of the word). In this 'theory' of the class struggle, which unfolds in a society divided into classes and in which the state is a specific instrument of the reproduction of this division into classes, there are, ultimately, no more classes for Gramsci, nor are there class struggles in the strict sense; there is what he calls a 'struggle of hegemonies', that is, a struggle between the hegemony of the dominant class and the hegemony of the dominated class.[10] Since the class struggle is thus thought as a 'struggle of hegemonies' (and since the critical-revolutionary moment is thought as a 'crisis of hegemony'), while the State itself is absorbed in the hegemony of the dominant class, everything happens between 'hegemonies', and *the question of the state finds itself practically and theoretically evacuated.* Put differently, while the question of the conquest of 'civil society' is clearly posed, and while it proves possible to propose an answer to it, a democratic answer, the question of the conquest of the state is, at bottom, not posed. It is not posed from the moment that the question of the state is thought in terms of hegemony, while the question of hegemony, in its turn, is thought in terms of civil society. This means that the question of the conquest of the state is not posed, since it is reduced to the conquest of civil society.

We have seen the extent to which Gramsci yields to the temptation to reduce one reality to another and substitute one question for another by devising the appropriate formulas. The most serious of these reductions, these substitutions, is the reduction of the state to civil society, the substitution of civil society for the state. This means, at the limit, that the question of the state is not posed in Gramsci's strategy; better, it means that the state does not really exist, since it is merely the phenomenon of hegemony.

All this conceptual 'labour' of so peculiar a kind was utilized by Togliatti in the sense everyone knows. He provided himself with the means of the strategy of the war of position by first laying the groundwork for a 'new party'[11]

Notes

Notes to Chapter 1

1 Vladimir Lenin, '*Kommunismus*', in Lenin, *Collected Works* (n.p.: Digital Reprints, 2012), www.marx2mao.com, vol. 31, p. 166. Mao Zedong cites this phrase in 'Strategy in China's Revolutionary War', in Mao, *Selected Works*, vol. 1 (Oxford: Pergamon Press, 1965, 3rd rpt, 1975), pp. 195–6, 251n.10, 'On Contradiction', ibid., pp. 323, 328, and 'Our Study and the Current Situation', *Selected Works*, vol. 3 (Peking: Foreign Language Press, 1967), p. 165. In all five passages, the English translation of Mao's rendition (具体地分析具体的情况) of Lenin's formula (конкретный анализ конкретной ситуации) reads 'concrete analysis of concrete conditions'.

2 Louis Althusser, *Reply to John Lewis*, in Althusser, *Essays in Self-Criticism*, trans. Grahame Lock (London: New Left Books, 1976), p. 49 and 49n.

3 'Dites-nous votre vie'. 'Nous voulons recueillir vos avis, solliciter votre participation à une large consultation, faire éclater la vérité sur votre vie quotidienne, la misère, les luttes, l'espoir.' 'Action, vérité, espoir: cent questions pour 30.000 réponses à *L'Humanité Dimanche*. Faisons connaissance' [Tell us your life. We want to collect your opinions, solicit your participation in a broad survey, and reveal the truth about your everyday lives, poverty, struggles, and hope. Action, truth, hope: One hundred questions and thirty thousand answers given to *L'Humanité Dimanche*. Let's get to know each other], *L'Humanité Dimanche*,

no. 49 (5–11 January 1977), cover and p. 2. 'For four weeks ... Communists in their hundreds of thousands are going to call on their neighbours and suggest that they depict their lives ... in "the ledgers of poverty and hope today". This is a kind of gigantic poll carried out by the French themselves ...'. 'Faire éclater la vérité et reculer l'injustice, déclare Georges Marchais' [Make truth burst into the light of day and make injustice retreat, declares Georges Marchais], *L'Humanité*, 7 January 1977, p. 4. See Louis Althusser, Letter of 8 February 197[7] to Hélène Rytmann, in Althusser, *Lettres à Hélène, 1947–1980*, ed. Olivier Corpet (Paris: Grasset/Imec, 2011), pp. 679–80.

4 '*L'Humanité* s'est fait quotidiennement l'écho des témoignages recueillis sur les cahiers de la misère et de l'espoir.' 'Incomparable témoignage sur la vie et l'espoir d'un peuple' [*L'Humanité* has daily echoed the testimony taken down in the ledgers of misery and hope. Incomparable testimony about a people's lives and hopes], *L'Humanité*, 14 February 1977, p. 1. The 'Poverty and Hope' campaign ran throughout 1977 and a little beyond.

5 A marginal annotation in Althusser's hand reads: 'It is not a matter of putting questions to people, but of getting them to think aloud: they *discover* things (during the interview) that they *did not know* they knew.' See p. 46 below.

6 Althusser is no doubt referring to the documentary film 'Appunti sul lavoro di fabbrica: una vita in fabbrica' [Notes on factory work: a life in the factory], filmed by RAI 2's 'Cronaca' television crew on Alfa Romeo's Arese-Portello site and first aired on 28 December 1977.

7 This phrase occurs in the report that Georges Marchais, General Secretary of the French Communist Party, delivered on 27 April 1978 to the Party's Central Committee. 'Georges Marchais: Avancer sur la voie du XXIIe Congrès' [Georges Marchais: Advance down the path of the Twenty-Second Congress], *L'Humanité*, 28 April 1978, p. 7.

8 Karl Marx and Friedrich Engels[, Moses Hess, Joseph Weydemeyer], *The German Ideology*, Marx and Engels Collected Works (hereafter MECW) (n.p.: Lawrence and Wishart Electric Book, 2010), 5, pp. 86–9; Marx and Engels, *Manifesto of the Communist Party*, MECW 6, pp. 492–3.

9   Karl Marx, *A Contribution to the Critique of Political Economy*, MECW 29, p. 24; Marx, *Theories of Surplus Value*, MECW 31, p. 467.

10 Marx and Engels, *Manifesto of the Communist Party*, pp. 490–1; Karl Marx, *Capital Volume One*, MECW 35, p. 366. Cf. Louis Althusser, 'Is it Simple to Be a Marxist in Philosophy?' in *Essays in Self-Criticism*, p. 203.

11 See Louis Althusser, *How to Be a Marxist in Philosophy*, ed. and trans. G. M. Goshgarian (London: Bloomington, 2017), p. 25.

12 Louis Althusser, 'Théorie marxiste et parti communiste' (unpublished ms., 1966–67), Imec, Fonds Althusser, Alt2. A07–01.10, p. 87; Althusser, *On the Reproduction of Capitalism: Ideology and Ideological State Apparatuses*, ed. Jacques Bidet, trans. Ben Brewster and G. M. Goshgarian (London: Verso, 2014), pp. 84n26, 188, 262; Althusser, *Philosophy for Non-Philosophers*, ed. and trans. G. M. Goshgarian (London: Bloomsbury, 2017), pp. 112, 192; Althusser, 'Philosophy and Marxism: Interview with Fernanda Navarro, 1984–1987', in Althusser, *Philosophy of the Encounter: Later Writings, 1978–1987*, ed. François Matheron and Olivier Corpet, trans. G. M. Goshgarian (London: Verso, 2006), p. 282.

13 The French word for body, *corps*, is also an equivalent of the English word 'corps', an ambiguity that Althusser exploits in 'Marx in His Limits', in ibid., pp. 101ff.

14 In the manuscript, the sentence is garbled; Althusser seems to have forgotten to strike the word(s) to be replaced by one of the two addenda he made to it. It might also be construed to mean 'they must be understood in their *body*, hence also in bodies, the activity of the body'.

15 Michel Foucault has demonstrated this very well, but using a different theoretical terminology owing to the fact that he has so far *avoided* posing the problem of the state, hence of the state ideological apparatuses, hence of ideology [Althusser's note].

16 The French word *syndicat* and the corresponding adjective *syndical* usually mean 'trade or labour union'. But they can be used, more broadly, of any association for the defence of common interests; thus, an employers' association can also call itself a *syndicat*. Althusser discusses the

implications in *On the Reproduction of Capitalism*, pp. 115–16.

17   See Louis Althusser, Letter of 25 October 1967 to Roberto Fernández Retamar, *Casa de las Américas*, no. 190 (January–March 1993), pp. 60ff.

18   'The Union of the People of France' was a formula that the PCF put into circulation around 1974. The Party's 1976 Twenty-Second Congress defined it as 'a large popular grouping ... of all the victims of the various forms of financial feudalism, *against* the narrow caste that dominates the country and is suffocating it, and *for* a democratic change that will deal this caste a severe blow by carrying out democratic reforms'. 'Georges Marchais: Avancer sur la voie du XXIIe Congrès', p. 9 (my translation).

19   The Union of the Left was an electoral alliance of the PCF, the Socialist Party, and the Movement of Left Radicals, a small party in the Socialists' orbit. In 1972, the three parties adopted a joint governmental programme, the *Programme commun* [Common Programme]. On the relationship between the Union of the Left and the Union of the People of France, see Louis Althusser, *Les Vaches noires: interview imaginaire (le malaise du XXIIe Congrès)*, ed. G. M. Goshgarian (Paris: Presses universitaires de France, 2016), pp. 449–50.

20   In this paragraph and the next, the words and phrases in inverted commas, many of them Communist Party slogans, are (sometimes loose) quotations from Georges Marchais' 27 April 1978 report to the Central Committee: 'Georges Marchais: Avancer sur la voie du XXIIe Congrès'. See above, n. 7.

21   Ibid., p. 10.

22   Althusser placed a footnote marker here without providing a footnote.

23   On 19 March 1978, in the aftermath of the 22 September 1977 rupture of the Union of the Left, the Right scored an unexpected victory in the second round of the French legislative elections, obtaining approximately fifty-one per cent of the votes cast.

24   The theory of State Monopoly Capitalism was effectively endorsed by the PCF at its 1967 Eighteenth Congress. Althusser elaborated a critique of it beginning in 1969, in

a series of texts most of which remain unpublished. His critique is summed up in Althusser, *Les Vaches noires*, pp. 391–414, and more briefly in Althusser, 'What Must Change in the Party', trans. Patrick Camiller, *New Left Review*, no. 109 (May–June 1978), pp. 35–7. See also chap. 3, n. 16.

25 The *Centre de diffusion du livre et de la presse* [Centre for the diffusion of books and the press] was a Party organization responsible for the sale and distribution of books and periodicals issued by publishing houses associated with the PCF.

26 This is a loose citation of Aristotle, *Metaphysics*, trans. W. D. Ross, in *The Basic Works of Aristotle*, ed. Richard McKeon (New York: Random House, 1941, rpt. 1968), 981b 28–29, p. 691: 'All men suppose what is called Wisdom to deal with the first causes and the principles of things'.

27 On the historical nature of the philosophy of praxis, see Antonio Gramsci, *Selections from the Prison Notebooks*, ed. and trans. Quintin Hoare and Geoffrey Nowell-Smith (New York: International Publishers, 1971), Notebook 11, §§52–54, §§58–59, §62, pp. 345–6, 364, 370, 373–4, 404–7, 411.

28 'The philosophy of praxis is absolute "historicism", the absolute secularisation and earthliness of thought, an absolute humanism of history.' Ibid., Notebook 11, §27, p. 465. '*Hegelian immanentism becomes historicism*, but it is absolute historicism only with the philosophy of praxis – absolute historicism or absolute humanism.' Ibid., Notebook 15, §61, p. 417.

Notes to Chapter 2

1 Palmiro Togliatti, *On Gramsci and Other Writings*, ed. and trans. Donald Sassoon (London: Lawrence and Wishart, 1979). With Antonio Gramsci, Togliatti was one of the founding members of the Italian Communist Party. He served as its Secretary General from 1947 to 1964.

2 Marx and Engels, *Manifesto of the Communist Party*, MECW 6, p. 487; Karl Marx, *Capital Volume Two*, MECW 36, pp. 43, 62. The German terms are *revolutionieren* and *umwälzen*.

3 On the use of 'relation of production' in the singular, see Louis Althusser, 'Book on Imperialism', in *History and Imperialism: Writings, 1963–1986*, ed. and trans. G. M. Goshgarian (Cambridge: Polity Press, 2019), pp. 76–9.

4 Ibid., pp. 134–6.

5 Louis Althusser, 'Letters to D.', Letter of 22 August 1966 to René Diatkine, in Althusser, *Writings on Psychoanalysis: Freud and Lacan*, eds. Olivier Corpet and François Matheron, trans. Jeffrey Mehlman (New York: Columbia University Press, 1999), pp. 62–3.

6 See Louis Althusser, 'To Gretzky', in Althusser, *History and Imperialism*, p. 42; Althusser, *Filosofía y marxismo: Entrevista de Fernanda Navarro* (Mexico City: Siglo XXI, 2015), pp. 74–5.

7 Louis Althusser, *For Marx*, trans. Ben Brewster (London: New Left Books, 1969), p. 146; Althusser, 'Union théorie/ pratique (deux premières rédactions)' (unpublished ms., 1966–67), Imec, Fonds Althusser, Alt2.A7–02.05, p. 16; Althusser, Letter of 25 October 1967 to Roberto Fernández Retamar, p. 5; Althusser, *Reply to John Lewis*, pp. 46–7.

8 According to Gramsci, 'the identity of history and philosophy' proposed by Croce 'remains incomplete if it does not also arrive at the identity of history and politics ... and ... thus also at the identity of politics and philosophy'. Antonio Gramsci, *Further Selections from the Prison Notebooks*, ed. and trans. Derek Boothman (Minneapolis: University of Minnesota Press, 1995), Notebook 10, Part 2, §2, p. 382.

9 Antonio Gramsci, *Prison Notebooks*, vol. 3, ed. and trans. Joseph A. Buttigieg (New York: Columbia University Press, 2007), Notebook 7, §24, pp. 173–6.

10 Nikolai Bukharin, *Historical Materialism: A System of Sociology*, trans. Alfred G. Mayer (translation of the 3rd Russian ed.) (Ann Arbor, MI: University of Michigan Press, 1969).

11 Gramsci, *Selections from the Prison Notebooks*, Notebook 7, §13–34, pp. 166–84.

12 Joseph Stalin, 'Address to the Graduates of the Red Army Academies' (1935), in Stalin, *Selected Writings* (New York: International Publishers, 1942), p. 365.

13   Gramsci, *Selections from the Prison Notebooks*, Notebook 11, §64, p. 371. See also ibid., Notebook 13, §18, p. 162.
14   Marx, *A Contribution to the Critique of Political Economy*, p. 263, translation modified to reflect Althusser's. The MECW translation has Marx affirming, about the 'conflict' between 'the material productive forces of society' and 'the existing relations of production', that 'men become conscious of this conflict and fight it out' in 'ideological forms'.
15   On the '"organic intellectuals" of the historical bloc', see Gramsci, *Selections from the Prison Notebooks*, Notebook 12, §1, pp. 5–23.
16   'The Roman church has always been the most vigorous in the struggle to prevent the "official" formation of two religions, one for the "intellectuals" and the other for the "simple souls".' Ibid., Notebook 11, §12, p. 328.
17   Ibid., Notebook 12, §1, pp. 17–18.
18   See Louis Althusser, '¿Existe en Marx una teoría de la religión?', in Althusser, *Nuevos escritos (la crisis del movimiento internacional frente à la teoría marxista)*, trans. Albert Roies Qui (Barcelona: Laia, 1978), pp. 166–7.
19   Several words near the right-hand margin of the page of the photocopy of the manuscript that begins here are too faint to read.
20   Althusser, 'What Must Change in the Party', pp. 39–40.
21   On the Risorgimento as an example of 'passive revolution', see Gramsci, *Selections from the Prison Notebooks*, Notebook 19, §24, pp. 55–63.
22   On fascism as an example of 'passive revolution', see ibid., Notebook 10, Part 1, §9, pp. 118–20.
23   Ibid., Notebook 13, §17, p. 106.
24   Marx, *A Contribution to the Critique of Political Economy*, p. 263. Althusser's quotations are approximate. In the MECW translation, the sentences he has in mind read 'No social formation is ever destroyed before all the productive forces for which it is sufficient have been developed' and 'Mankind thus inevitably sets itself only such tasks as it is able to solve'.
25   Althusser, *Reply to John Lewis*, p. 63.
26   Marx and Engels, *The German Ideology*, pp. 246, 437. Cf. 'The Humanist Controversy', in *The Humanist Controversy*

and Other Writings, 1966–1967, ed. François Matheron, trans. G. M. Goshgarian (London: Verso, 2003), p. 260.

27 See chap. 1, n. 28.

28 Althusser probably has in mind Marx's Letter of 27 June 1867 to Friedrich Engels, MECW 42, p. 390. See also Karl Marx, *Capital Volume Three*, MECW 37, p. 804.

29 This is an Althusserian variation on a Spinozist theme. See Benedict de Spinoza, *On the Improvement of the Understanding*, trans. R. H. M. Elwes, in *Ethics*, preceded by *On the Improvement of the Understanding*, ed. James Gutmann (New York: Hafner, 1963), p. 11, and Spinoza, *Ethics*, trans. William Hale White and Amelia Hutchinson, translation revised by A. H. Stirling, in ibid., p. 58, Part 1, Proposition XVII, Note.

30 Against such distinctions, Gramsci underscores the fact that the philosophy of praxis is, by its nature, an 'integral philosophy'. Gramsci, *Selections from the Prison Notebooks*, Notebook 11, §22, p. 435.

31 Vladimir Lenin, *Materialism and Empirio-Criticism: Critical Comments on a Reactionary Philosophy*, in Lenin, *Collected Works*, vol. 14, pp. 22–3, 40–7, 53–7, 63–5, 346–8, etc.

32 See Althusser, 'Can Everyone be a Philosopher?', in *How to Be a Marxist in Philosophy*, p. 145; Althusser, *Philosophy for Non-Philosophers*, pp. 23, 191–2; Althusser, *How to Be a Marxist in Philosophy*, pp. 10, 44, 127.

33 Karl Marx, 'Theses on Feuerbach', MECW 5, pp. 3–8. Marx does not use the word philosophy in 'Theses on Feuerbach'.

34 Ibid., p. 3. '[In Feuerbach], reality, sensuousness are conceived only in the form of the object, or of contemplation, but not as sensuous human activity, practice, not subjectively.'

35 Edmund Husserl, *Experience and Judgement: Investigations in a Genealogy of Logic*, ed. Ludwig Landgrebe, trans. James S. Churchill and Karl Ameriks (London: Routledge and Kegan Paul, 1973).

36 'Thus one arrives also at the equality of, or the equation between, "philosophy and politics", thought and action, that is, at a philosophy of praxis. Everything is political, even philosophy or philosophies ... and the only "philosophy" is history in action, life itself.' Gramsci, *Prison Notebooks*, vol. 3, Notebook 7, §35, p. 187.

37 On politics as the first moment of the superstructure, see Gramsci, *Selections from the Prison Notebooks*, Notebook 13, §10, p. 137.

38 'Archimedes sought but one firm and immovable point in order to move the entire earth from one place to another. Just so, great things are also to be hoped for if I succeed in finding just one thing, however slight, that is certain and unshaken.' René Descartes, *Meditations, Objections, and Replies*, ed. and trans. Roger Ariew and Donald Cress (Indianapolis, IN: Hackett, 2006), p. 13. 'You are looking, like Archimedes, for a fixed point in order to lift up the world, and you think you can find it in this principle or statement: I think.' Pierre Gassendi, 'Recensement des arguments nouveaux contenus dans les instances de Gassendi', in Descartes, *Œuvres philosophiques*, ed. A. Garnier, vol. 2 (Paris: Hachette, 1834), p. 509 (my translation). See Althusser, 'Is it Simple to Be a Marxist in Philosophy?', p. 183; Althusser, 'Marx and History', in *History and Imperialism*, p. 155.

39 Marx, 'Theses on Feuerbach', p. 8.

40 'State does not mean only the apparatus of government but also the "private" apparatus of hegemony or civil society.' Gramsci, *Prison Notebooks*, vol. 3, Notebook 6, §137, p. 108. Criticizing the notion of the state as 'night-watchman', Gramsci shows that the state must include elements of civil society. Hence the famous equation 'state = political society + civil society' (ibid., Notebook 6, §88, p. 75). For more on the critique of the state as 'night-watchman', see Gramsci, *Selections from the Prison Notebooks*, Notebook 26, §6, p. 262. For a 'watchman' definition [*una definizione* 'veilleur'] of the state, see [Antonio Gramsci, *Quaderni del carcere*, ed. Valentino Gerratana (Turin: Einaudi, 1975)], §10, p. 1465. [The preceding sentence is a handwritten addendum. There is nothing about the state on the page cited.]

41 G. W. F. Hegel, *Elements of the Philosophy of Right*, ed. Allen W. Wood, trans. H. B. Nisbet (Cambridge: Cambridge University Press, 1991), §189ff., pp. 227ff.

42 'What we can do, for the moment, is to fix two major superstructural "levels": the one that can be called "civil society", that is the ensemble of organisms commonly called "private", and that of "political society" or "the

state". These two levels correspond on the one hand to the function of "hegemony" which the dominant group exercises throughout society and on the other hand to that of "direct domination" or command expressed in the state and "'juridical" government.' Gramsci, *Selections from the Prison Notebooks*, Notebook 12, §1, p. 12, translation slightly modified to reflect Althusser's. The published English translation reads 'command exercised through the State and "juridical" government'. The Italian reads 'comando che si esprime nello Stato e nel governo "giuridico"' (Gramsci, *Quaderni*, vol. 3, pp. 1518–19).

43   Jean-Jacques Rousseau, *The Social Contract, or Principles of Political Right*, trans. Willmoore Kendall (Washington, DC: Regnery, 2009), p. 22.

44   The combat tank regiment stationed in the small town of Rambouillet, about thirty miles south-west of Paris, went on manoeuvres in the forest nearby during the May 1968 events.

45   See Althusser, *On the Reproduction of Capitalism*, p. 197n32.

46   Ibid., pp. 74, 242.

47   Gramsci, *Selections from the Prison Notebooks*, Notebook 11, §27, p. 462; Gramsci, *Further Selections from the Prison Notebooks*, Notebook 10, Part 1, §13, pp. 360–1.

48   Karl Marx, *The Eighteenth Brumaire of Louis Bonaparte*, MECW 11, p. 193 note b.

49   Gramsci, *Prison Notebooks*, vol. 3, Notebook 7, §16, p. 169.

50   'The massive structures of the modern democracies, both as State organisations, and as complexes of associations in civil society, constitute for the art of politics as it were the "trenches" and the permanent fortifications of the front in the war of position: they render merely "partial" the element of movement which before used to be "the whole" of war, etc.' Gramsci, *Selections from the Prison Notebooks*, Notebook 13, §7, p. 243.

51   Paul Laurent, 'Graves propos de Louis Althusser' [Alarming remarks of Louis Althusser's], *L'Humanité*, 13 May 1978, p. 1. I have replaced a blank in the manuscript with the date of the article, in which Laurent, a member of the PCF's secretariat, vehemently attacks Althusser. His immediate

target is an interview in which Althusser sharply criticizes the Party's leadership, mode of functioning and organization, and political line ('Al "punto zero" della teoria: Louis Althusser ha avviato nel Pcf un severo dibattito autocritico sulle ragioni della sconfitta elettorale' [At the 'degree zero' of theory: Louis Althusser has initiated a serious self-critical debate in the PCF about the reasons for the electoral defeat']), interview conducted by Giorgio Fanti, *Paese sera*, 6 May 1978, p. 5. 'Communists will judge the attack launched by Louis Althusser ... as it deserves to be judged. That is why they will take action to ensure that the undertaking of which it is a part is completely foiled' (my translations). See also chap. 1, n. 23 and chap. 3, n. 16.

52 This is an allusion to comments made by a member of the PCF leadership, Charles Fiterman, on an article in *Le Monde* about Althusser's criticism of the Party's decision, taken at its February 1976 Twenty-Second Congress, to abandon the concept of the dictatorship of the proletariat: 'Honestly now, from Giscard d'Estaing through *Le Monde* to Roger Garaudy, a curious front of partisans of the dictatorship of the proletariat is shaping up. The handful of comrades who continue to cling adamantly to certain texts while losing sight of the living soul of Marxism are not the swallow of the spring of which our adversaries have been dreaming for fifty years – a spring that has never seen the light of day and never will. These comrades will reflect on matters and we will help them.' 'À propos d'un article du *Monde*. Charles Fiterman: Rien ne nous détournera de notre combat' [On an article in *Le Monde*: Charles Fiterman: 'Nothing will divert us from our combat'], *L'Humanité*, 26 April 1976, p. 5 (my translation).

53 Althusser, *On the Reproduction of Capitalism*, pp. 243, 252–3, 268.

54 Friedrich Engels, Letter of 21–22 September 1890 to Joseph Bloch, MECW 49, p. 34; Engels, Letter of 25 September 1895 to W. Borgius, MECW 50, pp. 265–6, translation modified to reflect Althusser's.

Notes to Chapter 3

1 Cf. Gramsci, *Selections from the Prison Notebooks*, Notebook 13, §20–§21, pp. 133–6, esp. p. 136; pp. 147–8.

2 Nicolò Machiavelli, *Discourses on Livy*, trans. Harvey C. Mansfield and Nathan Tarcov (Chicago, IL: University of Chicago Press, 1996), pp. 29, 36.

3 Niccolò Machiavelli, *The Prince*, 2d ed., eds. Quentin Skinner and Russell Price, trans. Price (Cambridge: Cambridge University Press, 2019), pp. 26, 29–33, 56–8, 75.

4 Ibid., pp. 59–60.

5 Ibid., pp. 60, 67.

6 Ibid., pp. 21–2, translation modified to reflect Althusser's.

7 Ibid., pp. 60–1.

8 Ibid., pp. 61, 62, 77.

9 Machiavelli, *Discourses on Livy*, pp. 34–5, 41–4, 285–7.

10 Niccolò Machiavelli, *The Art of War*, in *The Essential Writings of Machiavelli*, ed. and trans. Peter Constantine (New York: The Modern Library, 2007), pp. 296–305.

11 Claude Lefort, *Le travail de l'œuvre: Machiavel* (Paris: Gallimard, 1986 [1972]), pp. 725ff.

12 Machiavelli, *The Prince*, p. 19, translation modified to reflect Althusser's. The Italian is 'questo evento di diventare di privato principe'.

13 Ibid., pp. 53, 66; *Discourses on Livy*, pp. 214–15.

14 Althusser, 'The Humanist Controversy', pp. 238ff; Althusser, 'Marx's Relation to Hegel', trans. Ben Brewster, in Althusser, *Politics and History: Montesquieu, Rousseau, Hegel, Marx* (London: New Left Books, 1972), pp. 182ff; Althusser, *Reply to John Lewis*, pp. 94–9; Althusser, 'Book on Imperialism', pp. 117–20; Althusser, 'Marx and History', in ibid., pp. 147–8.

15 Machiavelli, *The Prince*, p. 53.

16 Between 24 and 27 April, Althusser published a four-part article in *Le Monde* (issues dated 25, 26, 27 and 28 April) highly critical of the French Communist Party ('Ce qui ne peut plus durer dans le Parti communiste français', translated into English as 'What Must Change in the Party'). In his 27 April 1978 report to the Party's Central Committee, Georges Marchais took note of this critique, in his fashion, and of the fact that it had appeared in the non-Party press: 'Does this deliberate neglect of the collective debate in the Party not testify to a fear of seeing his personal political positions rejected by the majority after a free discussion?

It's true that it's easier to hold monologues seated behind a desk and to write peremptory monologues that have no trouble finding takers' ('Georges Marchais: Avancer sur la voie du XXIIe Congrès', p. 7). Althusser riposted in an expanded version of his *Le Monde* articles published as a small book in May: 'When it comes to monologues and desks, the [Party] leadership has nothing to learn from anybody' (Althusser, *Ce qui ne peut plus durer dans le Parti communiste français* [Paris: Maspero, 1978], p. 11) (my translations). Cf. Althusser, *The Future Lasts Forever*, trans. Richard Veasey (London: Chatto & Windus, 1993), p. 170.

17 Machiavelli, *The Prince*, pp. 35–6, 61.
18 See p. 71 and n. 34 below.
19 Machiavelli, *The Prince*, pp. 85–8.
20 Ibid., pp. 23, 26–9.
21 Ibid., pp. 60–1.
22 René Descartes, *A Discourse on Method*, in *A Discourse on Method, Meditations on the First Philosophy, Principles of Philosophy*, trans. John Veitch (London: Dent, 1975), p. 16.
23 Althusser, 'Is it Simple to Be a Marxist in Philosophy?', p. 170; Althusser, *Machiavelli and Us*, ed. François Matheron, trans. Gregory Elliott (London: Verso, 1999), pp. 29, 56, 99.
24 Machiavelli, *Discourses on Livy*, p. 15.
25 Machiavelli, *The Prince*, p. 20.
26 Ibid., p. 85, translation modified to reflect Althusser's.
27 Machiavelli, *Discourses on Livy*, p. 13; Machiavelli, *The Prince*, p. 18.
28 Ibid., p. 53, translation modified to reflect Althusser's.
29 See Althusser, *On the Reproduction of Capitalism*, pp. 77–8, 138–9, 155–7.
30 Karl Marx, 'Notebooks on Epicurean Philosophy', MECW 1, p. 492; Marx and Engels, *The German Ideology*, p. 28.
31 Machiavelli, *The Prince*, p. 4, translation modified to reflect Althusser's.
32 Ibid., p. 21.
33 Ibid., p. 77.
34 Nicolò Machiavelli, *The History of Florence*, in *The History of Florence and Other Selections*, ed. Myron P.

Gilmore, trans. Judith A. Rawson (New York: Twayne Publishers, 1970), pp. 137ff.

35 Here at least one line is missing at the top of a poorly photocopied page.

36 Machiavelli, *The History of Florence*, Book 3, chap. 12; Machiavelli, *Discourses on Livy*, pp. 16, 18.

37 Ibid., pp. 19, 78; Machiavelli, *The Prince*, p. 34.

38 Ibid.

39 Machiavelli, *Discourses on Livy*, pp. 18–19.

40 Here at least one line is missing at the top of a poorly photocopied page.

41 Gramsci, *Selections from the Prison Notebooks*, Notebook 13, §20, p. 134.

42 See Althusser, 'The Humanist Controversy', p. 296.

43 Cf. Louis Althusser, 'Machiavelli's Solitude' (1977), trans. Ben Brewster, in Althusser, *Machiavelli and Us*, p. 118: '*The Prince* and the *Discourses*, now 350 years old'. As Althusser himself points out, Machiavelli 'signed off' *The Prince* in 1513 (ibid., p. 21).

44 Here at least one line is missing at the top of a poorly photocopied page.

45 Three illegible words in Althusser's handwriting appear opposite this sentence in the margin of the manuscript.

Notes to Chapter 4

1 'The parties that have together been described as "Eurocommunist" ... all affirm the same determination to advance towards socialism by struggling for the continued progress of democracy in all fields on the basis of broad popular alliances, while respecting pluralism and rejecting all notion of a model.' Laurent, 'Graves propos de Louis Althusser', p. 1 (my translation).

2 See Althusser, *Machiavelli and Us*, pp. 63–4, 88–9.

3 See Althusser, *Les Vaches noires*, p. 148, 148n3.

4 Althusser's expression, *les pays de l'Est*, usually designates the Eastern European countries. Cf. 'in the USSR and the other countries of the East' below.

5 This argument is developed in Althusser, *Les Vaches noires*, pp. 141–5.

6 'Résolution [of the PCF's Twenty-Second Congress]', *Cahiers du communisme*, February–March 1976, p. 387.

See Althusser, *Les Vaches noires*, p. 445; Althusser, 'On the Twenty-Second Congress of the French Communist Party', trans. Ben Brewster, *New Left Review*, no. 104 (July–August 1977), p. 1: 'The document adopted by the Congress is … not a concrete analysis of a concrete situation … but a … *Manifesto,* expounding to the French people … "the society the Communists want for France: socialism".'

7   On 3 June 1976, Berlinguer and Marchais held a big 'Eurocommunist' rally in Paris. They met again in Rome on 29 April 1977.

8   See Santiago Carrillo, *Eurocommunism and the State*, trans. Nan Green and A.M. Elliott (Westport, CT: Lawrence, Hill & Co., 1978). Carrillo, General Secretary of the Spanish Communist Party, received Marchais and Berlinguer in Madrid on 2 March 1977. 'An event the importance of which can be neither glossed over nor minimized …': 'Berlinguer, Carrillo, Marchais à Madrid', *L'Humanité*, 3 March 1977, p. 1.

9   See chap. 1, n. 20.

10 See chap. 2, n. 47.

11 The text breaks off here.

Index